The
Dog
Walker

The
Dog
Walker

**AN ANARCHIST'S ENCOUNTERS WITH
THE GOOD, THE BAD, AND THE CANINE**

Joshua Stephens

MELVILLE HOUSE
BROOKLYN · LONDON

THE DOG WALKER

First Melville House Printing: September 2015

Melville House Publishing   8 Blackstock Mews
    145 Plymouth Street   and   Islington
    Brooklyn, NY 11201   London N4 2BT

mhpbooks.com   facebook.com/mhpbooks   @melvillehouse

Library of Congress Cataloging-in-Publication Data
Stephens, Joshua, author.
The dog walker : an anarchist's encounters with the good, the
bad, and the canine / Joshua Stephens. — 1st ed.
    pages   cm
    ISBN 978-1-61219-451-6 (hardcover)
    ISBN 978-1-61219-452-3 (ebook)
    1. Stephens, Joshua.   2. Dog walking—Biography.   3. Dog
walking—Anecdotes.   4. Dog owners—Washington (D.C.)—
Anecdotes.   5. Anarchists—Washington (D.C.)—Biography.
6. Political activists—Washington (D.C.)—Biography.
7. Human-animal relationships—Washington (D.C.)—Anecdotes.
8. Washington (D.C.)—Social life and customs—21st century.
9. Social stratification—Washington (D.C.)—Anecdotes.
10. Washington (D.C.)—Biography.   I. Title.

SF427.46.S74 2015
636.70092—dc23
[B]
                                                           2015032674

Design by Marina Drukman

Printed in the United States of America
        10 9 8 7 6 5 4 3 2 1

*For Blake, an anarchist
and once dog walker who, given
the opportunity, would've
written a far smarter, far funnier
book than this one*

Contents

Introduction

This book began (in earnest, anyway) in a vegan restaurant off Manhattan's Union Square, over a dinner marking my thirty-sixth birthday. Seated at the table that night was sometimes anarchist academic James Birmingham who, in keeping with the conventions of such occasions, inquired as to whether I was ever going to do anything with the idea of writing about my time as a dog walker.

"Didn't you do some interview with *The Washington Post* or something?" he asked.

It didn't really have anything to do with writing a book, but he wasn't wrong.

In 2011, the style section had run a story on a worker-cooperative dog-walking agency I'd cofounded back in 2006. Having already relocated from D.C. to Brooklyn, I'd initially only seen the web version. But further into the day, seated in Madison Square Park's dog run, next to a handful of what looked like soccer moms busy rehearsing two-syllable, outer-borough-accented pronunciations of the word *whore*, I noticed someone fingering through the print edition. I was shocked to find that the story had somehow made the front page of the A-section. Above the fold.

Below the fold was the latest on New York congressman Anthony Weiner, who was resigning from office after tweeting his barely concealed penis to some young woman—and thereafter, the *world*. And then, for some time after the image was leaked, bewildering everyone by pretending he couldn't place the obvious piece of side-pipe staring back at him. By the time *The Washington Post* had come knocking, I'd actually already left the dog-walking cooperative in question. But even so, I had taken some joy in the *Post*'s layout that day. Top story: Anarchists provide proof-of-concept. Also in the news: disgraced, politically reprehensible politician falls victim to (a) own horrible decisions and (b) cock quips.

Joining us at the table that night was Jay Cassano, a freelance journalist covering technology and social movements. He'd come into my life more recently, and had never heard me say a word about the book idea. Jay reminded me of our mutual friend's (then) fiancé, who works at the publishing house that would eventually get behind this book. But even this bit of insider info failed to stir me in any immediate way. Coasting on four years of lazy, idea-stage inertia, I shrugged, and returned to what seemed the far more pressing matter of shoveling strawberry shortcake into my face.

Remarkably, against all likely odds, here we are. What you're holding in your hands prevailed against both my nonexistent at-

tention span and New York City's unparalleled vegan dessert offer-
ings. I'm still sort of shocked no one beat me to the punch. Someone
sharper, more enterprising—at the very least, more proactive. Dog
walkers, after all, are a cultural institution—and they've steadily
become more and more visible in the developed world. An urban
scene for a film or TV show can scarcely be staged without an ex-
tra cast as one, passing in the background. There's a built-in intelligibility to dog walkers—a set of automatic assumptions. They
signify—correctly or not—various features of urban (and, more
and more, *suburban*) life. Conspicuous consumption. The quaint
priorities of aging Gen Xers who've graduated to professional life
and have begun to hire Millennials, who themselves are scraping
by amid the diminishing returns of artistic pursuits. These angles
aren't wrong, exactly, but the authentic aspect of the trade they tend
to capture is superficial at best.

As adult professionals increasingly postpone having families,
dogs have become "starter children," and thus dog walkers feature
in everyday life much as babysitters have for generations—though
with virtually none of the broad familiarity or detailed rendering.
While nanny diaries fly off shelves and make for blockbuster cinema
(and this is after decades of cultural dominance by the Baby-Sitters
Club) and bike couriers receive both action-film and reality-TV
treatments, the urban figure nestled between, who in many ways
combines the salient features of the two, slips in and out of frame
in the background, not unnoticed, but nonetheless unknown. This
opacity—a kind of incompleteness of perspective—conceals two

very rich narratives. The first: the (often ethically questionable) antics one can get up to when one has unfettered access to the lives of others, combined with relative anonymity; the second: just how many of our secrets and stories are known by these relatively anonymous figures.

Also, there is poop. And animals mounting one another's faces in front of small children.

It'd have been easy enough to pack my story with navel-gazing reflections on the contrast between conventional careers and healthy priorities à la Oprah, or Gwyneth Paltrow, or some other bright-eyed lifestyle charlatan. I know this because such sentiments were buried in the refrain of virtually every liberal-minded *actual* adult who ever inquired as to what I did for a living. It was always a nakedly vicarious and invariably unsettling sort of approval, with a predictable refrain nestled somewhere within it: find something you love and do it for the rest of your life. And if you can weave in some cute animals, so much the better. They'll enrich your experience, bring you back to the simple things in life, and remind you not to sweat the small stuff.

Someone somewhere is bound to write that book.

This is not that book.

In fact, it's my quiet hope to preemptively torpedo the authority of such an effort. Because there's a lot more to this story—to this life—than the warm wishes and charmed fantasies of strangers. Dog walking, after all, is a line of work. Like all work, the social, political, and economic backdrop against which it unfolds *matters*.

Not only does that matter, I'm convinced that it's far more compelling to any reader than, say, what I learned from gazing into the eyes of a retarded corgi, or how many times I jerked off in the homes of congressional staffers.

I wouldn't wish some book full of tears and pithy life lessons on *anyone*. I certainly wouldn't write the thing. Which is not to say dog walking didn't teach me a great deal. It most definitely *did*. Further, it afforded me enough quiet and introspection to fully investigate what I was both learning and *witnessing*. An unfortunate side effect of quiet and introspection, however, is that when most people acquire any quantity of either, they squander it, simply by assuming it's a product of their own unique grit and determination; as if they deserve it more than anyone else does. I'd like the record to reflect that I did not deserve it *at all*. My years as a dog walker thus served as a sort of master class in the practice of gratitude. And in giving some account of those years, I've tried to convey something nominally less assholish than the self-convinced entrepreneurial "insight" such a book would typically give center stage. I've tried to say something at least worth the time someone won't get back, having read it.

Then again, I'm terrible at most things. So . . . no promises.

What you're about to read is a selection of field notes. The conventional memoir format seemed a poor fit, inasmuch as my life just isn't that interesting, and wasn't likely to be made more so by committing it to chronologically accurate exposition. I've opted, instead, to represent the experience exactly as I had it: as a series of vignettes through which I saw refracted any number of human experiences, mostly unrelated if not for the fact that they occurred and intersected at the feet of a dog walker. A dog walker who happened to have a particular politics, and a corresponding FBI file. Within these stories, I've sought to weave a fairly detailed view of what the trade entails. How a workday spent in the elements collides with various seasons. What it feels like to work in and around the front lines of gentrification, before developers have had a chance to move in the yoga studios some focus group has indicated are a vital ambient comfort to white women. What it means to fall in love with *place*. How work can be a crucible for prefiguring new ways of being together. The practical and emotional skill sets required in servicing human-animal relationships, left of frame for the casual observer.

Mostly, I've tried to do justice to what I still believe is probably the greatest job in the world, for all that it gave me, and all it enabled and provoked me to do. Enjoy.

The
Dog
Walker

1

REVERSE-INDEXING SMUG, SABER-RATTLING SHITHEADS, OR HOW I BECAME AN ANARCHIST

I had Spanish first period the day the United States began bombing Iraq in 1991. Or rather, I was *supposed* to. Instead, my teacher arranged the desks in a circle and staged what was probably a well-meaning but ill-advised group therapy session. As it happened, we were less than a thousand miles from Baghdad, on a U.S. naval air station. The one from which the airstrikes were being staged. So it arguably had a bit more weight than it might've otherwise.

Here's what I remember about the awkward fifty minutes we spent together that day:

1. It was readily apparent our teacher had grossly overestimated the emotional and intellectual sophistication of a room full of teenagers. She had expected adolescents socialized within the U.S. military to need the space to "process," but for that to be true, said

adolescents would've had to access any perspective whatsoever on events that contrasted with those beamed through U.S. military media. *And* they'd have had to give a shit. Mere mention of the fact the United States had backed Saddam Hussein (even through his worst crimes—the United States had *increased* weapons transfers after he gassed his own people) would've likely led to at least one or two students spontaneously combusting, or left janitors cleaning adolescent brain fragments off the windows. It was, as it was destined to be, anticlimactic. The usual, inherited platitudes were expressed, ambivalence was feigned lest anyone's vanity suffer for their evident, unquestioning indifference. Hair was twirled.

2. The exception, here, was the one girl who stared straight ahead, silently but evidently horrified. Her father was a pilot. But she was mostly sidelined by the one junior naïve enough to play grown-up by dating an enlisted guy; in our social world, this was an Icarus-esque kiss of death for one's romantic or sexual prospects among one's *actual* peers. Being *that* girl made you untouchable, inasmuch as everyone knew you were sleeping with someone who almost certainly frequented brothels in the corner of Catania known as The Gut. She sat sobbing, not over her lackluster judgment, but as an overcompensating performance of the higher stakes of her "adult" relationship.

3. The impact Desert Storm might have on Iraqis was never mentioned.

I was thirteen. I don't claim to have had a terribly robust or dynamic politics, but the first album I bought with my own money, at age ten, was Anthrax's *Among the Living*, which happened to include songs about militarism and the genocide of Native Americans. By the time the first Gulf War kicked off, I'd moved on to punk rock, and was not squeamish about saying that—regardless of whatever "complexity" upon which adults in my midst insisted—raining bombs down on people was a terrible idea. I'd also recently seen George Carlin's stand-up routine about not believing *anything* the government said, nor, for that matter, anything reported by the corporate media (the only media I really *had*), which was in Carlin's estimation merely an unofficial PR wing of the State. All of this was more formative for me than one might imagine; every conversation I encountered about the war now felt incomplete at best—or, more often, like total bullshit. I was imparted with an unapologetic confidence in withholding trust from State actors and advocates, alike.

So when, a few weeks later, the same Spanish teacher showed us some segment from *Good Morning America* or the like, about how Peter Cetera (famous front man of eighties hit factory, Chicago—as well as the man behind that epic theme song to *The Karate Kid 2*) had a songwriting partner who'd penned a protroop anthem titled "Voices That Care," I had no patience for any of it. Within a few weeks, she'd used some elaborate MS-DOS function to produce a dot-matrix-printed banner with the song's chorus, which she had the class hang for soldiers passing through the base's air station. By the spring, the administration forced the school's chorus (a class: performances were a factor in students' grades) to sing it at an evening event for parents and the extended base community. This struck me as ironic. We'd actively targeted the Amiriyah shelter for women and children with missiles, in the name of publicly spanking some tyrant to whom we'd previously provided serious financial and military aid—and to underscore the nobility of the gesture, students in my school were given a choice: literally sing its praises, or risk failing a class. Why bother assigning Orwell, really?

Thankfully, I wasn't *in* the chorus class. But some of my classmates in other courses were. When I queried them one day about whether or not they felt put upon at being forced to cheerlead the bombing of school buses and ambulances, or the use of tanks to bury people alive in the desert, I was shouted down and threatened within an inch of my life in front of our English teacher—an older woman married to a Sicilian, mostly helpless to make sense of navy brats, much less control them. As we crowded out of class, I was shoved down the stairs.

When historians and political philosophers distinguish the fascism of World War II Europe from conventional totalitarianism, the key ingredient is typically that the former was not simply imposed from above. There was a popular, grassroots animus. A *micropolitics*; what Gilles Deleuze and Félix Guattari described as a fascism of the province, of the town, of the village, or of the household. In the case of Germany, anti-Semitism. In Spain and Italy, national identity. All of which held militarism in highest esteem. Little is more demonstrative of the intellectual and moral bankruptcy of elected officials than their lip service to the military as the "best" our culture has to offer. Its version of community life was the crucible of my adolescence, and I owe it the ease with which I absorbed Deleuze and Guattari's notoriously painful writing, when it came to fascism.

Each day of my high-school years, as the sun dipped, the flags would be lowered at the front gate of the base, and "Taps" would be played through a loudspeaker nearby. Anyone outdoors, within earshot, was expected to stop, face the front gate, remove any hat, and remain still for the duration of the ritual. Not only those in uniform. *Everyone.* And they policed each other, to ensure compliance. I was routinely chastised by middle-aged uniformed men for continuing to skateboard at various sites around the base as they stood at attention; none of them was terribly enthused to hear me reply (usually over my shoulder) that *they* had made the choice to join up, not me, and that that was how the freedom-cookie crumbled. To this day, the previews at movie screenings in base theaters operated by the U.S. military are preceded by a playing of the national anthem, for which all moviegoers—including children—are required to stand. In a fucking movie theater. One *not* in 1930s Nuremberg.

The racism and jingoism I saw pervading the military community—even among spouses and children—was appalling. The expressed attitudes toward local nationals (in this case, Sicilians) were as abhorrent as they were unapologetic. U.S. minorities weren't off-limits, either—despite that they populated the enlisted ranks in considerable numbers. Jokes about black men found at the bottom of lakes, having "stole[n] more chain than they could swim with" were not uncommon. At a quasi-medieval-themed dinner venue where my mom was dining with officers and representatives of private-sector military systems providers, I was grilled by the wife of a commander with a (half-drunken) "But don't you think Jesus would really enrich your interest in social concerns?" in virtually the same moment that her husband responded—annoyed—to a performance by dancers in ambiguously "eastern" dress with "Didn't we colonize those people?" These attitudes, as shit is wont to, rolled downhill to my peers. Many ducked back into the military as soon as they graduated—perhaps simply because they knew nothing else, and the contrast of the outside world was more than anyone had prepared them for. Some now work as privately contracted mercenaries. When the Abu Ghraib story broke in 2004, I was reasonably confident I went to high school with someone involved.

Writing in the preface to Deleuze and Guattari's *Anti-Oedipus*, Michel Foucault asked, "How do we rid our speech and our acts, our hearts and our pleasures, of fascism . . . the fascism that is ingrained in our behavior?" In 1991, I'd never heard of any of the aforementioned thinkers, but that question was probably, in some form or another, the defining feature of my adolescence. In that oh-so-crucial phase of teenage individuation, I was desperately clawing my way to whatever positioned me as far as possible from the example in which I was immersed. Clumsily. With incredibly mixed, not altogether flattering, results. The first day of "spirit week" my sophomore year was "bum day," in which every adult in a position to intervene and stage a teachable moment (including the Spanish teacher) failed to bat a lash at an entire student body dressed as caricatures of the poor and homeless, replete with "will work for food" signs. When "country and western day" rolled around and I turned up dressed as a Klansman, they were suddenly—remarkably— possessed of an attention to the dangers of stereotypes, and duly unenthused.

I'm shocking no one by relaying that clashing with that culture at every turn didn't play well for me. It went rather badly, in fact. After a few years, I was diagnosed with chronic stress headaches so severe that my mom actually let me quit high school, on the condition I immediately obtain a GED and enroll in college classes. But even surviving for that long required the acquisition of a number of skills. Very early on, I discovered that—rather mysteriously—having a better command of information and argument seemed to diffuse situations. Especially situations in which I was likely to get my ass kicked. Teachers would intervene, perhaps out of some sense of obligation to uphold a "use your words" approach to life's hiccups. Peers would (usually) back down, perhaps because the obvious temper tantrum of pummeling someone who'd out-argued them wasn't something they wanted on their tacit social CV. Who knows? All that matters is that I noticed. And I set about arming myself.

This didn't, however, equip me with any sense of where to begin. The Internet didn't exist. I was stranded in the middle of the Mediterranean, in a country whose language I did not speak well enough at that point to seek out resources locally. The base library was not exactly brimming with Chomsky, nor would I have had much means by which to know why he mattered. Instead, I mentally catalogued everything I'd ever heard an officer or defense contractor shit on or disdain, and then I sought out its literature. I figured that if a particular idea or concept or cultural form had riled such people, I probably stood to learn something useful from it. I was seldom let down.

For a time, that process was pretty radically constrained by what was on offer around me. I had Thoreau and Enlightenment philosophy as a counter to the evangelical Christianity bombarding me at every turn; feminist literature to interrogate the version of masculinity valorized by military culture and a home life shot through with domestic abuse; Hesse and Gibran to make alienation less terrifying; MLK and "Eastern" philosophy to assure the radically defiant possibilities embedded in discipline. All of which was roundly ridiculed, resented, or worse, by every intellectually bankrupt asshole positioned to exemplify "adulthood" for me. I skipped classes almost daily and holed up in the library, reading. I found my way to local Marxist squats and social centers in the city and began frequenting them, language barrier be damned. But beyond these few pinholes into the world and what I'd memorized from punk record sleeves, I had little to work from.

Until, that is, I started hanging out with this girl in Rome. My mom was away for work, leaving me home alone during spring break. My tax return from a summer job had shown up, and our landlord—a likely mafioso eager to pilot light any adolescent mischief in which I showed interest—explained how to reserve a sleeper bunk on the train and wake up eight hours north. With my mom poorly positioned to intervene, I locked up the apartment and hit the road. And so began a semiregular routine of taking the overnight train up on Friday nights, spending Saturday nights at punk shows in squatted castles and other such spaces, all the while nursing a crush on a girl who may or may not have had any such interest in me, before crashing on the train home Sunday nights.

During one of our outings in Rome, I discovered two fanzines published out of the Netherlands and Germany, *Burial* and *Counter-Clockwise*, respectively. Both espoused a trifecta of straightedge (a punk discipline of firm sobriety), veganism, and communism—an ideological cocktail popularized by Dutch hardcore band Manliftingbanner. I'd long adopted the first two prongs on that trident, but the third was pretty much the holy grail—an unmistakable "fuck you" to the tacit culture of the military, a scant half-decade out of the Cold War. And so I dove in, treating the essays and interviews in those zines like a bibliography, seeking out every thinker or book mentioned.

In short order, my early exit from high school became an expedited parting of ways with military myopia. With a semester's worth of college credits under my belt to soften the blow of my GED, I fled stateside, ultimately landing at American University in D.C., a city I'd long coveted for its disproportionately influential punk history. Once there, my college years didn't last long, either. Starved for years of real contact with the very things from which I'd drawn the inspiration to merely *survive* my adolescence, punk shows and grassroots organizing consistently proved irresistible, felt more vital, and monopolized my attention.

My first proper summer living in D.C., the group house I'd just moved out of—a student house on the George Washington University campus, near the corner of Twenty-Second and G Streets NW where I'd illegally rented a second-floor sunroom—was effectively running the city's premier underground show venue out of its basement. Pretty much every small punk and hardcore act touring that summer passed through. Shows happened almost nightly. A local straightedge kid by the name of Doug Wordell had just returned from his first year at Evergreen in Olympia, Washington. We were introduced by my first solid friend in D.C., an indefatigable—and barely eighteen—vegan activist named Paul Shapiro; now the vice president of farm animal protection at the Humane Society of the United States. We sat out one of the bands one night, retreating to the steps of the School Without Walls, around the corner. Doug was one of the few straightedge kids I'd met in the United States who gave a shit about anything political, and I was eager to bond. I was surprised to discover his first year in Olympia had turned him on to anarchism—until that point, I'd mostly thought of it as the nihilistic free for all it denotes in the popular imagination. I pushed back, arguing for more conventional—and in my mind, more structured—Marxist politics. He quoted Russian revolutionary Mikhail Bakunin to me. "Liberty without socialism is privilege, injustice. Socialism without liberty is slavery and brutality." It was the first inkling I ever got that anarchism repre-

sented something more than a naïve political application of chaos
theory.

One day, browsing a bookshelf at the Positive Force collective
house in Arlington, I came across Russian geographer and natural-
ist Peter Kropotkin's pamphlet *Anarchism and Anarchist Communism*, and recognized his name as one Doug had mentioned. To say
that the book broke everything open for me would be to undersell
it, dramatically. It was practically a religious experience. A majority of the practical questions and contradictions I'd been grappling
with in my own politics dissolved. I quickly sought out and de-
voured anarchist texts with the same vigor that had animated my
hours in the library back in Sicily. Whereas Marxism took as its
object of analysis the matter of *exploitation*, the anarchist tradition
took aim at *domination*. White supremacy. Patriarchy. Colonialism.
Militarism. Capitalism. The State. Self-styled "Marxist" regimes
had—as anarchists like Kropotkin had predicted—reinscribed the
very authoritarianism they'd fought to take down, rationalizing
antidemocratic institutions as a foil to exploitation. For anarchists,
no such deal with the devil was necessary. Direct democracy was
possible. Cooperation was possible. Self-organization was possible.
Socialism from the bottom up was not only possible, but *necessary*.
Community self-determination replaced the aspirations of elec-
toral politics or authoritarian States. Beyond being dynamic and
flexible, anarchism implied an ethics; it was imminently *practicable*, in the now, embodied best perhaps in the works of German
anarchist and sometimes Jewish mystic, Gustav Landauer. "The

State is a condition, a certain relationship between human beings, a mode of behavior; we destroy it by contracting other relationships, by behaving differently toward one another," he famously wrote in an essay titled "Anarchic Thoughts on Anarchism," perhaps anticipating Foucault taking aim at the fascism ingrained in our behavior. "We are the State and we shall continue to be the State until we have created the institutions that form a real community."

Everything came full circle, for me. And I never recovered. There was no grand narrative, no "after the revolution." There was simply what we do in the here and the now. Anarchism was the aspiration at the core of radical democracy, cooperation, and compassion—present as much in Ella Baker's work in the civil rights movement as in the history of Spanish resistance to fascism prior to World War II. And therein was equally a holistic orientation of the self, with deeply *emotional* significance. "We are not in the least afraid of ruins," wrote Spanish anarchist militia leader Buenaventura Durruti, during the civil war provoked by Francisco Franco's fascist uprising. Now well into my thirties, the sentiment feels keenly *existential*, sufficient time having elapsed to accumulate my own share of *personal* defeats; those places where we're forced to continue after the story driving our life at a particular moment has ended against our will (perhaps for a second or third time). Relationships that come apart, careers derailed, family or community tragedies. Being in the world necessarily inheres surveying one's own ruins, from time to time. There's something of a litmus test buried in Durruti's insistence: do we really mean it—politically, spiritually, emotionally—if we forfeit the game at the prospect of ruins? Durruti's refusal of fatalistic cynicism (perhaps unwittingly) blurred the lines between spiritual and political life; especially the case for our present moment, faced with overwhelming suffering and myriad looming crises. Not least of which are ecological ones. "The bourgeoisie might blast and ruin its own world before it leaves the stage of history," he wrote. "We carry a new world here, in our hearts. That world is growing in this minute."

Every bit as much as anarchism represented, for me, a fierce lack of romance for existing political institutions and social organization, it also held a—perhaps unrivaled—infatuation with *possibility*. And that possibility was contingent on little more than initiative and a moment-to-moment commitment to exercising power *with*, rather than power *over*.

If nothing else, it's a combination with a far lower body count than the aspirations normalized for me, in high school. It certainly made looking in the mirror easier.

2

WALKING, WE ASK

The Zapatistas—the indigenous rebels of southeastern Mexico, forced onto the world stage by the rollout of NAFTA on New Year's Day 1994—are one of the most playful, literary resistance movements in history. Their communiqués usually read as much like Borges as they do Guevara, and they often convey their core community aspirations through almost overly earnest proverbs. Their once primary spokesperson, an iconic, pipe-smoking *ladino* widely known as Subcomandante Marcos, penned a children's book about diversity in which he described sex as "a good way to get sleepy before a nap," and he's frequently issued declarations through re-counted dialogues with a talking beetle named Don Durito. In 2008, while I was attending a Spanish immersion program at the *centro de lenguas* operated within one of movement's autonomous municipalities, my *promotore* (Zapatistas are quick to reject im-plicitly hierarchical binaries like teacher/student or doctor/patient, and thus have only "promoters"—of education, of health, of food, etc.) offered a shortcut for remembering that Spanish nouns ending in *ion* are always accompanied by the female article, deploying a cheeky, feminist wink-nudge: "*El problemo es masculino; la solucion es feminina.*"

I'd traveled to Chiapas (the home-state of the rebellion, near the border with Guatemala) in part as an attempt at nominal professional development. *As a dog walker.* My work routine required me to key into the homes of people who typically hired cleaning services staffed by Spanish-speaking immigrants. Many of these folks had rarely encountered dogs that were not tethered to uniformed men with guns, and they were often visibly ill at ease with my four-footed charges. Returning from a walk to find cleaning staff in a client's home, I'd usually fumble my way through abysmal Spanish and improvised hand gestures, offering to put the dog(s) in another room while they finished, in the hopes of making their job a little less frustrating. It occurred to me that we shared a certain class-commonality in being employed by the same people. All comforts of a potential connection were, of course, promptly undermined by the fact that I could speak to our employers with much greater ease.

It's not that I had any illusions about how *very* different our lives were. It simply seemed reasonable to care enough about those differences to—at *minimum*—say, "When we cross paths, let's meet where *you're* most comfortable." I don't know whether that had any value or meaning to anyone but me, but the practice of *seeing* others, being present with them—of meeting people on terms other than those dictated to us—was, at the very least, freely available. Certainly, it felt less shameful than doing nothing. So: Spanish immersion in the context of a rebel movement "for humanity, against neoliberalism." Plus, it was an excuse to expense a six-week jaunt through Chiapas and Oaxaca come tax-time.

The cab ride up the mountain from the colonial, tourist-saturated town of San Cristóbal de las Casas into *territorio Zapatista* took about an hour. As a backpack-bedecked gringo, traipsing beyond the tourist *andador* and standing head and shoulders above locals in the open-air market on the town's outskirts, I was spotted by cabbies pretty quickly. "*Oventic?! Oventic?!*"—the apparent destination for anyone moving through the neighborhood with my complexion and attire. All of this felt somehow abstract and visceral at the same time. Here were taxi drivers—a fairly mundane fixture of almost any urban environment—offering to take me to a place that still felt about as real to me as Narnia. Prior to the 1994 uprising that seized the town, stranding tourists and torching property records, the Mexican military had stumbled onto a Zapatista training camp in the jungle, effectively confirming hushed rumors of a looming indigenous insurgency. Under normal circumstances, the discovery likely would've sounded all sorts of alarms and triggered a sizable military response (as the uprising itself eventually did), but this was Mexico pre–NAFTA, when the agreement was still being negotiated. Given the stakes, the government moved swiftly to quash all talk of anything destabilizing in the indigenous south, dismissing it as mere fable or hearsay. Today, virtually every tourist

shop in the town sells postcards immortalizing an iconic moment
in the uprising: Zapatista insurgents, slouched against a wall in the
town center, beneath graffiti echoing the repeated proclamation of
the then president—*No hay guerilla*—"There are no guerillas."

Some part of me still hadn't fully metabolized that phrase's fal-
lacy. Getting in a cab felt like climbing into a spaceship.

My arrival at the autonomous *caracol*, or community, where the
school sat nestled was unceremonious and abrupt. Trees befitting
the more urban terrain turned to pines jutting through low-slung
clouds, and switchbacks blurred together until suddenly they didn't.
The taxi stopped, I craned my neck to see through the windshield,
orienting myself by the only industrial, reflective road sign in our
vicinity. It read: PARA TODOS TODO. NADA PARA NOSOTROS.
("Everything for everyone. Nothing for ourselves.") I stepped out
of the cab across a nondescript road toward a makeshift gate of cor-
rugated steel, watched over by a woman of less than five feet who
sported a ski mask, a rifle, and a shoulder-slung infant. A badly
behaved Weimaraner—those lanky, silvery dogs often featured in
TV commercials—weaved his way between us, tracking through
a mist-moistened mud. The woman scolded him with little effect,
clearly resigned to the annoyance, as I presented her with my initial
entry documents.

Once beyond the gate, I was escorted to the *oficina de vigilan-
cia*, to register as a guest with the community's governing council.
The Weimaraner, undeterred and clearly well practiced at evading
all half-hearted, exasperated admonitions, had trailed us down the

hill and followed us indoors, as though he were as much a part of the formality as anyone else. As soon as he was noticed, a minor fracas ensued, with ski-masked farmers attempting to wrap arms around the wiry dog and haul him out, with all the clumsiness of a first-ever attempt. Mud smearing on denim, paws spinning and dragging across concrete. Not wanting to presume I knew better how to manage the local canine troublemaker, I smiled appreciatively and watched. After a full five minutes of wrangling, the dog got bored and moved on.

"*Como se llama usted?*"

"Josue."

"*Y donde vive?*"

"Washington, D.C."

"*Y su trabajo?*"

"*Yo trabajo cuidando perros.*" ("I work watching dogs.")

In advance of my trip, a Chilean friend I'd hired as a tutor advised me this was the most succinct way of describing my occupation, though the sheer demand for such labor was so geographically and culturally distinct the phrase went little distance in making any sense of what I did. Truth be told, what I did for a living made little sense to *me*, in that moment. A journalist had once told me of her initial visit to the community, standing next to a bonfire her first night, chatting with a man probably in his seventies. After asking where she was from, he'd inquired as to how far she'd traveled. "Six hours flying, huh?" he mulled her answer, pensively. "And how long *walking*?" Certainly, to the most impoverished population on the continent—among whom literacy was a product of tangible, even grave, struggle—the description of an activity like walking dogs around a city as remunerative *work* was more likely to yield eye-crossing and astonished contempt than any real meaning. Given what had just transpired, and the two men in front of me still catching their breath, I suddenly realized I appeared to be making a joke. "I work watching you jackasses wrestle with dogs." I bristled for an instant, worried I'd inadvertently mocked them, before seeing their eyes soften through their ski masks as laughter ripped through the room.

While they recovered, I broke the levity. *"En serio. Es mi trabajo. Yo camino con los perros de los ricos."* And so my registration with the community was completed: gringos are so awash in cash that some asshole actually made his living entertaining their dogs. And that asshole had a face. I was off to a good start.

The origin story of the Zapatistas involves a *foco*—a term used by Che Guevara to denote a core group of revolutionaries who foment rebellion in a broader population. In this case, Marxist-Leninists who traveled south from Mexico City in the early eighties to sow revolt among the oppressed indigenous. There is, of course, no shortage of leftist chauvinism in such aspirations—what James Baldwin called "the fraud and folly of good intentions." Upon arriving in the jungles of Chiapas, this *foco* was confronted with their outsider status. The CliffsNotes of the story might go: "What you ladinos are proposing sounds fine, but in case you haven't noticed . . . we have our own history, our own communal and political practices. If we're gonna do this, it's going to be on our terms, and with us in the driver's seat." In short, a narrative in which a strict sense of self-determination is absolutely paramount.

Alongside that primacy is a certain immediacy: a self-determination that requires an unfolding awareness of—if not responsiveness to—existing conditions. Prior to the events of New Year's 1994, Zapatista communities experienced what they call "the first rebellion"—an organized refusal by women to ratify *any* community decision until a series of demands around gender equality were met. The result was the Women's Revolutionary Law, a document that stipulates women's rights to reproductive choice, collective economic self-determination, and among other things, communal sobriety as a material bulwark against domestic violence. It should thus come as little surprise that, among the many proverbs circulating in *Zapatismo*, one finds the phrase *"Caminando, preguntamos"*—"Walking, we ask [questions]." Its meaning is twofold: movement, but with an agile humility and curiosity—interrogating all things, not least oneself. It suggests a critical attention to what's immediate to one's experience, putting it in conversation with broader realities. In the equation this proverb sets up, movement is not dependent upon *answering* questions. It is simply aided by their asking. When the young woman leading my course on women and Zapatismo was asked how a community agreement ensuring reproductive choice is reconciled with widespread Catholicism and its corresponding antipathy toward contraception (even within the rebel movement), she replied without hesitation: *"Es un proceso."*

"It's a process." As though a belief that such transformations in people's hearts could be exacted in less than twenty years was an absurd delusion. What was at work was not a self-sure determination of will ultimately manifested in some cataclysmic toppling of this or that institution, but an orientation against inertia. What it requires is a comfort with and commitment to open questions, one that exposes how institutions can speak through us long after we've overthrown them.

It's a sentiment that resonates, still, for me. At the risk of seeming trite, I want to suggest a more literal reading, in light of this book's subject matter. Walking confers real *time* for asking questions, in a manner most activities do not. Having done it professionally, I know this in my bones—for better or worse. Walking is an activity that offers fewer distractions with each increase in volume. It is exceedingly difficult to escape oneself or one's circumstances, moving at such a pace. Dilemmas, the sweetness of memory and the joys of possibility, the shame of our shortcomings and the sadness of loss, the banality and the novelty of the everyday—it all draws into crisp, sometimes unbearable focus. I would argue that it's amid all of this that questions of real consequence even occur to us.

There's also the matter of walking as a dislocation, an interstitial state of being; *between* places, between references or narratives. Often, without realizing it, we nominate later moments or milestones for the deferral of particular questions. The bridges we opt to cross once we've come to them. We'll entertain the connection and demands of loving fully once we've "found" ourselves, or acquired this or that insight about our lives. We'll travel once we've banked some quantity of years at a given job, or built the necessary CV for one later one. Even the manner in which many of us hang so much of our well-being on careers in which we have negligible (and steadily decreasing) control—our healthcare, our long term material stability—at some point suggests a pattern of deferment that borders on pathological.

Key in this subtle, inherited calculus is the distinction of arrival. Time spent in motion becomes null, impotent—even wasted, or counted against productive or meaningful activity, as though it cancels our capacities or as though what we do with it is of no consequence. Often enough, it's not clear we even regard it as our own. We appear to have gleaned, almost in spite of ourselves, that the means of producing our own joy have been foreclosed, stolen off to be bought back. It's not merely a macropolitical carrot-stick narrative; it's become how we understand ourselves. And it is, despite whatever spin we give it, ultimately little more than a refusal to *begin*. As though we are not on borrowed time, as though everything we acquire in the not-walking moments will not be taken away from us (likely by the whim of a boss, a landlord, or some or another "market correction"—well before death claims what's left)—and as though we can know in this moment that we will be better equipped in some later one. Better to focus on arrival and resolution, we say. We assume questions cannot or will not remain open, or evolve, or be subject to revision; we assume we are exempt from having to live with or within them. The impulse against beginning *where we are* is as persistent as it is seductive. And, in addition to it being incoherent, irrational, and politically unpalatable in the abstract, it is—consequentially speaking—categorically *insane*.

Working as a dog walker inverted this conventional approach to time and movement for me, with rote precision. Walking was not a matter of reaching pursuits, the speed with which it carried me between them. Quite the opposite; it was effectively irreducible. I was tasked with *filling time* with motion undertaken for its own sake. A half-hour walk simply needed to be a half hour of walking. It largely did not matter where that took me, or how I minimized interstitial time between moments of presumed greater significance. In turn, what I did with that time *became* significant. It's not that I sought to be more economizing, making use of dead time, like a kid opting to study during detention. I simply stopped seeing time as empty or dormant, and began to show up more fully to everything that happened. Architecture. Seasons. City sounds. Coffee. Living things. Strangers. Dog walking was a daily repeated exercise in contesting a vision of life that is, at its core, contemptuous of *living*.

We should be embracing open questions; relishing what is unresolved. Both represent ideal terrain for experimentation. And ideally, the questions we ask in the in-between spaces ought to be predominantly *social* questions; questions that interrogate fiercely the options presented to us—*all of us*; questions that ask us to imagine other possible lives, and the conditions most likely to bolster them. Not self-soothing daydreams that drown out what hurts or overwhelms us, but what Brazil's landless workers' movement describes as "expanding the floor of our cage until the bars can no longer contain it." Not merely politically, but emotionally; how we show up for each other, and the surfaces against which that occurs. And not merely questions about what's possible, but on how to bring other possibilities into being. The here to there. The mechanics.

I could've been any number of things. Many more conventionally understood to be ripe with transformative possibilities. But the clock was ticking, and I happened to be a dog walker. We begin where we are. One foot in front of the other. As we are. Without recourse to some later, more optimal moment or qualification. However imperfect this moment may be.

Un proceso.

Walking.

With questions.

3

A PEOPLE'S HISTORY OF PROFESSIONAL DOG WALKING

A few words on dog-walking history.

Most available material traces the first professional dog-walking outfit to Jim Buck, the son of a well-to-do family on Manhattan's Upper East Side. Buck shows up in newspaper articles everywhere from *The New York Times* to *The Times* of London. They all more or less tell the same story. In his adolescence, he'd shown dogs, and later spent a good deal of time training horses on a farm run by his family in Connecticut, a trade he took to with apparent zeal and considerable talent—enough to land himself an invitation to audition for the U.S. equestrian team in the lead-up to the Rome Olympics. According to a short 1965 profile in *The New Yorker*, he had to decline. "By then I'd done what was expected of me, and gone to work downtown," he said; after stints in shipping and other areas, he eventually wound up the vice president of a small electronics firm.

His wife, Ann, was born into a hotel family, and had spent time around dogs as a kid. Predictably, she and Jim eventually had dogs of their own. "I discovered soon enough that I preferred walking them and the neighbors' dogs in Central Park to putting on my tie and getting downtown to the office," he told *The New Yorker*. "But it didn't occur to me to go professional and forget about downtown until I stumbled on the realization that a Great Dane can be trained exactly like a show horse." So was born Jim Buck's School for Dogs, in 1964, which would cater to the dogs of Manhattan's well-heeled for the next four decades, until Buck's retirement. Along the way, he hired as many as two dozen "assistants," mostly recruited by word of mouth at Upper East Side cocktail parties, mostly former equestriennes who'd landed in the city chasing careers in model-ing, nursing, or as airline stewardesses. Much as Buck had him-self, they found repurposing horse-training skills as dog walkers preferable to their various professional environs. Understandably. Some pulled in as much as five hundred dollars a week, a not alto-gether terrible haul for an agency dog walker, even by contempo-rary standards.

Buck's story has been *the* origin story for the trade ever since, revived in various international obituaries upon his death in 2013. And one can understand why. The son of an Upper East Side family who passed on college life in favor of an apprenticeship in an elite recreation; his shot at Olympic glory stymied by the pressure of con-vention and the obligation to enter professional life; vice president by his early thirties, despite little more than a high-school diploma. All this, only to then forsake all his inherited luck and access, Buddha-like, to pass the next forty years as a fedora'd dandy quasi-celebrity who wore through his soles every two weeks, allegedly keeping a certain cobbler in business. All hail the genius of the uptown golden boy, whose entrepreneurial tenacity saw him identify a gap in the market that he then successfully exploited. Buck thrived while discreetly servicing the gilded, and gave distinction to what was effectively manual labor. It's about as textbook an Upper East Side fairy tale as one can imagine.

The problem is, it's not *true*. Or, at least, it's not the origin story of dog walking. Apparently, no one who wrote about Buck at *The New York Times* ever bothered to check their own archives. If they had, they'd have come across a headline in their January 5, 1935, edition, which reads "WALKING THE DOG NOW BIG BUSINESS." A thirty-four-year-old building super on West Seventy-Fourth Street named James Daley was days from opening an office on Broadway, north of Columbus Circle, out of which he was running Daily Dogwalking Service, Inc., offering daily dog walks for five dollars a month. Daley had observed clearly annoyed husbands sent out by their wives, who'd have "rather read the last chapter of a detective story late at night than act as a nurse for a frolicsome canine." So he dispatched "porters, chambermaids, elevator operators, even his own wife" to perform the task in their stead. In many parts of the world, this is still more the norm than a designated walker, but Daley saw in it a task that could be managed by one outfit, across multiple buildings—across the *country* eventually, he hoped. "I'm the originator," he told the *Times*. "It was my idea. I couldn't sleep nights, sometimes, thinking about it."

It turns out that *this* is not entirely true, either. While Daley had taken a decidedly professional approach to the trade—even devising plans for liability insurance to cover death, injury, or the loss of a dog in the care of his walkers—the construction of the service goes further back, still. That is, at least according to yet *another* story in the paper of record. The previous year, the *Times* apparently ruled newsworthy that the dean of Barnard College, Virginia C. Gildersleeve, had decreed that the students she'd been paying fifty cents an hour for the last three years to look after her Cairn terrier, Culag, would be subject to new regulations to accommodate the dog's advanced age. (Lest you scoff at fifty cents, by the way, it was a figure based on going rates for childcare at the time. Then again, maybe you should still scoff.) "The dog is to be exercised for an hour in the morning, generally from 10 to 11," read the original rules. "I allow a few minutes leeway at the beginning or end of the hour for class purposes, but think he should be out at least fifty minutes. In the afternoon he is to be walked for forty minutes from 3 to 3:40 and then cleaned and brushed for a quarter of an hour." The new rules stipulated that Culag should not be forced into "violent exercise," or dragged "against his inclination."

Why any of this was worthy of column space in *The New York Times*, I have no idea. But it suggests that professional dog walking was happening at least as early as 1931, and was eyed as a scalable industry with national franchising possibilities by 1935. It also suggests that its professionalization as a designated trade had its roots not with a flamboyant son of fortune—but, more likely, with working-class folks who'd cleaved it off from various jobs into which it had been traditionally folded.

History. Written by the victors. Or the rich kids protesting, "No, no. It's not manual labor. It's repurposed *equestrianism*." Right.

4

ANY PORT IN A STORM

"Mmmm. I *love* chest hair." Her hand traced the gap between my collarbones, then snaked up around the back of my neck, settling in the half-assed haircut a friend had given me in Pittsburgh the week prior. The words poured out in a postcoital purr so clichéd I almost cringed. They weren't helped by the fact that the stated preference seemed unlikely. In the two-and-a-half days we'd known each other, she'd been pretty forthcoming about her lifelong lesbianism. I couldn't tell if I were being humored in some clumsy attempt at pillow talk, or witnessing a personal reassessment well out of proportion with our germinal rapport.

The sun was still up, beating through the windows of her Westfalia, where we lay tangled in hastily shed clothes on a foldout bed, trespassing in some stranger's cornfield. Nowhere, Minnesota. An impromptu "rest stop," the purpose of which was plain to the both of us, without so much as a word. She was making her way home to Olympia from an eastward solo road trip through Canada. I was undertaking a short-lived and ill-advised move to Seattle after a crushing breakup and a yearlong torrent of shitty news. I'd set out from D.C. for some anarchist conference in Louisville, planning to meet a ride to the West Coast from there. The weekend came and went, without any sign of or word from my ride. Faced with being stranded in Louisville, I accepted a friend's offer of passage to his place four hours north in Pittsburgh, and spent the next week in a university computer lab, pinging contacts to coordinate my way out. I was about a day from booking a flight when a friend referred me to a woman he'd met at some gathering at the Institute for Social Ecology (a now defunct, sort of anarchist college) in Vermont, who was about to drive west across the United States. "You're welcome to ride with me!" she wrote back. "One catch: *You'll need to meet me in Pittsburgh.*"

It was a welcome, if unlikely, bit of serendipity. The preceding nine months had taken such a toll that I'd developed a bit of an eating disorder I'd miraculously hid from everyone around me. It had the unfortunate side effect of occasional hypoglycemic fits that less occasionally resulted in fainting. The most recent such incident had occurred after standing still for the twenty minutes it took my friend to finish the aforementioned haircut. He graciously peeled me off the floor, force-fed me, and took me on a walk. On better days, I headed off such embarrassment with Charlie Chaplain-esque attempts at normalcy, like propping myself upright using the counter of a Chinese take-out joint, as a date and I waited for food. I was threadbare, running on fumes.

Staring at the ceiling of the Westfalia, still damp with the sweat of my impromptu travel companion, I traced the chain of events up to that moment. More likely than not, I was a regrettable exception for her, made in a moment of intense disorientation. The morning prior to our tryst—our first in each other's company—began in sleeping bags on the living-room floor of a house in Bowling Green, Ohio, where the anarchist magazine *Clamor* was published. "You guys should get up," one of the editors said, waking us. "Someone's flying passenger jets into the World Trade Center."

By the time I reached Seattle, the economy was in a free fall. Coming from D.C., a city whose primary economic engine was the one institution unlikely to come unglued anytime soon, I was accustomed to there always being *some* odd thing I could get paid to do, in a pinch. Peers were known to pull in considerable hourly rates line-standing for lobbyists at various congressional offices, for instance, and the larger labor unions typically had budgets to hire people to cause trouble for business-friendly efforts on Capitol Hill—disrupting some sham panel, or a hearing, or what have you. I once made a day's work of delivering to congressional offices cookies decorated as pie charts of defense versus all other discretionary spending, and farting in as many of them as I could manage. In Seattle, I was generally overqualified for each of the ten jobs I applied to daily, and never received as much as a confirmation e-mail in reply. Worse, the friend who'd invited me out, who had dangled the "spare room" in his house as a surefire residence, had neglected to run it by any of his housemates. It turned out that some of them were rather firm in their belief that the TV room should remain the TV room. Unemployed, broke, and facing the prospect of hunting for housing in a city I barely knew, I fired off three resumes to nonprofit jobs back in D.C. one day, mostly out of exhaustion and half-hearted curiosity. Within half an hour, I had replies from all of them, and I immediately gave myself till the end of the month before I left. In the interim, the ex with whom I'd split flew out to reconcile, sealing the deal. Almost two years to the day, we'd be married. By the time I left, I had lasted all of about eight weeks in Seattle.

When I stepped off the plane at Dulles mid-November, still destroyed, with the added humiliation of a failed escape attempt under my belt, I had thirty-five cents in my pocket. I was reasonably confident I'd find work in another nonprofit. Though only *eventually*. Such things always took time, even with well-placed contacts, and in the interim, I'd settle for any shitty retail gig I could nail down. I loathed the idea, but I had little choice. I'd deliberately set out to keep my return as quiet as possible, but my first morning back, I surfaced at a café staffed by a longtime friend, unable to decline food, now making a conscious effort to treat my body a little less terribly. It was there, slouched over the classifieds of the *Washington City Paper*, that I paused at an ad for a position with a small dog-walking agency.

Can You Show Me How to Dougie?

The first professional dog walker I'd met was a guy I'll call Dougie. We were introduced in what was then a parking lot on the corner of Thirteenth and U Streets NW, across from Ben's Chili Bowl—one of D.C.'s longest-standing cultural landmarks. It was June 1999. I was twenty-one. At the time, I'd just returned from an underwhelming antiwar conference in The Hague; my most enduring memories were that I'd chickened out of dropping twenty-five dollars to watch a live sex act in some seedy Amsterdam dive at the last minute, and had skipped the cost of housing by camping in The Hague's main park for a full week. At home, I had been working two or three days as an administrative assistant at an animal rights organization alongside several overnights each week at a small church-run haven for homeless women. The evenings I wasn't there were mostly spent reading in an over-air-conditioned basement apartment near American University, rented from a sweaty, mouth-breathing latter-day Marlon Brando, prone to drunken misdials that resulted in answering machine inquiries about "mother-daughter combos."

I'd recently been convicted alongside twelve other folks on federal charges of "invading the property of a foreign government" and named by said foreign governments' cartoonish daily newspaper as a "terrorist" on retainer with both the CIA *and* the Vatican. That latter bit would've been convenient, if true, as none of what I was up to at that moment paid terribly well. My life was a headlong dive into coupling moral outrage with punk-rock irreverence, in which long-term stability figured mostly as trite; quaint, on a good day. I could've been stuck working retail or (god help me) food service, and instead, I had more free time than I really deserved; raw material from which to cultivate a not inconsiderable annoyance for various institutions.

Dougie, by comparison, struck me as exceedingly normal. There was something unsettling about it; like he was a brazen imposter in circles saturated in a seriousness for which he had little use and to which he felt little obligation. I'd guessed him probably a decade or more my senior. He was stocky, had given up fighting his thinning crown, and exuded a joviality that seemed a fitting accompaniment to his rosy, cherubic features. Committed as he seemed to be, he looked an unlikely activist. His overall presentation was that of a vaguely bearish gay man, with none of the corresponding fashion sense. I'd abandoned any guesses about his sexuality upon discovering that he frequently left the house in sweatpants; a move I (only *half*-jokingly) declared a white flag of existential surrender— like sitting down in the shower. It was not uncommon for him to circulate videos from a campfire on some farm, decked out in his signature sweats, a warmer version of a Members Only jacket, and a clashing knit cap with earflaps, belting out a capella folk songs just as likely Balkan as Appalachian. He thus became, over the years, especially for other friends of mine who knew of him, a sort of cartoon character, and (no doubt exaggerated) tales of his antics were a routine and celebrated feature of our conversations.

However comically absurd he appeared on the surface, it went

without saying that he was, by comparison, far and away the better human being. And likely the happier, as well. Whereas Dougie
embodied a sort of childlike, wide-eyed curiosity and absolute lack
of pretension, my circles were hopelessly self-serious, despite still
being mostly populated by adolescent dickheads. However noble
our cause(s), we were still only a few years away from a distinctly
juvenile lack of judgment. Just a week prior to my meeting Dougie, I'd regaled my tent mates in the Zuiderpark with an arguable
low point of my adolescence in Sicily: an incident in which I'd ass-
slapped an elderly widow decked out in the traditional black, from
the anonymous comfort of a passing car. "Congratulations," one
of them replied. "You're officially the *eighth* person I know who is
definitely going to Hell."

Dougie and I crossed paths that day in 1999 for the purposes
of a carpool into rural Virginia. We were both attending a training camp in direct-action protest tactics organized by the Ruckus
Society, on a former tobacco plantation. If you've ever seen activists hang like rock climbers from a building, dangling a banner,
or seen people locked to concrete-filled buckets to stop a pipeline
or an arms shipment—odds aren't terrible that they were trained
by Ruckus. You typically don't just learn these kinds of things by
improvising. Back in the late nineties, these camps were happening
every few months, free of charge to anyone whose application was
accepted, thanks to considerable funding somehow coaxed out of
Ted Turner (yes, that Ted Turner), who apparently fancied himself
an environmentalist, for some brief moment. A few months after

this particular training, however, Ruckus played a central coordinating role in the minor November uprising that shut down the World Trade Organization's ministerial in Seattle, and kicked off several years of antiglobalization upheavals. Turner had, it turned out, a much more substantial romance for free-trade agreements than he did the natural world or its inhabitants, and he promptly pulled all funding for Ruckus, curtailing their activity considerably.

Over dinner our first night at the camp, Dougie bonded with a guy from New York who wouldn't have been out of place in the cast of *Clerks*. He looked more likely to hold forth on what hockey fights feel like after huffing gas than anything in which I might've been remotely interested. But there he was, attending camp as part of a group practically at war with Rudolph Giuliani over the mayor's seizure of community gardens on Manhattan's Lower East Side. The bulk of his conversation with Dougie circled around their shared line of work: accompanying dogs around each's respective city. I'd been aware the occupation existed, but had sort of assumed it was a negligible rarity; a unicorn gig that doubled as a punch line enabled by First World frivolity. Hockey Fights admitted he moonlighted thrifting cigar boxes from shops on pregentrification St. Mark's and then selling them on eBay as "vintage," but it seemed unlikely from his description that this could amount to a primary income. His tone suggested there was nothing terribly remarkable about the fact that he was making a proper and comfortable *living* leading groups of dogs around Lower Manhattan. I studied Dougie's responses, expecting some disbelief, but he instead chimed in with his own shoptalk, waxing jubilant about the critters, the clients, and the truncated work hours this all involved.

I was enraptured. I'd only been back in the United States four years, and this revelation left me feeling as though fairly major features of my environment had eluded me. Had these two weirdos really managed to short-circuit the parameters of making a comfortable living? They clearly weren't working terribly *hard*—nor had this coup they'd pulled off come by way of any disproportionate insight or planning. It was as though they'd just fallen ass-backward into it, oblivious to its novelty. Like, "Yeah. I'm a professional doughnut eater. It's no big deal."

Becoming Mr. Right Now

My call to the number in the classified ad was followed by an interview, in a house on the far, western side of the Mt. Pleasant neighborhood, half a block out of Rock Creek Park; a sort of unsculpted valley-forest that cuts vertically through the northwest quadrant of D.C. From the outside, anyway, there aren't a lot of shitty houses in Mt. Pleasant. That said, this one seemed slightly out of reach for a thirty-something single mother running a pet-care agency out of her kitchen extension. Especially since the business had recently been split with her ex-husband in a divorce. The house may have been acquired similarly, come to think of it, though I never asked. The setting seemed a bit too polished for the sort of revenue I suspected she was pulling in with a staff of four. My skepticism

was mostly down to having not fully grasped what it was I was stepping into.

Much like narcotics, dog walking is effectively *all* margins. Its
operating overhead is very nearly negligible, limited both by its
labor-intensiveness and lack of transparency. Urban neighborhoods
are dense enough—and traversing them flanked by four or more
dogs is conspicuous enough—that visibility and marketing are
practically built-in. Word of mouth is, in many cases, perfectly sufficient. The liability insurance James Daley had sought to institute
in the thirties, now very much a reality, figures mostly as an au-
thenticating luxury; a "look, Ma, I'm a real business!" accessory. No
licensing or certification is required—in nearly a hundred years no
oversight agency has seen fit to become sufficiently dexterous with
the industry's terms or moving parts to regulate it. Additionally,
the rate at which these outfits generate revenue increases not in in-
crements, but exponents. A single thirty-minute Monday-to-Friday
client amounts to an annual gross of $5,000 to 8,000, depending on
local price points, and one is typically working that in a multiple of
three or four at any given point. All of this in a workday that can
last as long as six hours. It is, once one hits a critical mass of clients,
breathtakingly lucrative.

It was even more lucrative if you ran half the business off the
books, as my would-be boss was doing. This was not at all uncommon, and it illustrates perfectly the anything-goes quality of the
trade. In theory, at least, the relative lack of operating overhead has
the downside, when running a business legitimately, of yielding

comparably few tax write-offs. The incentive to hide revenue, and the means at one's disposal in such an already informal and obscure trade, ought to be self-evident. The whole thing felt keenly illicit, and yet there seemed little indication that any state actor who ought to give a fuck was doing any such thing. Even now, about the only way one could really get any sense of how the industry's grown, where it's grown, or who's working in it is through the membership rolls of the two industry associations that cater to it—Pet Sitters International, and the National Association of Professional Petsitters—neither of whom answer their phones, return calls, or reply to e-mails. As far as I've ever been able to tell.

I all but waved her off when the boss mentioned a trial period. "It's not for everyone. It's incredibly physical. People have quit after a single day." Bold, given that I'd just turned twenty-four weighing in at what I had at puberty, and only in the preceding month or so resumed eating with any regularity. Hired on the spot, I left that day with a six-month commitment and little intention of staying in the business. Frankly, I had little respect for it, as work. It seemed almost unspeakably quaint. Aside from the rather dire necessity of income, I was mostly there out of what seemed a fairly finite curiosity. The initial, relative mysteriousness made it enticing, but as *work* it seemed an embarrassing admission. I dove in with the hope that some quantity of fleeting adventure might be in the cards before I had to scuttle back into office environs. There was an off-the-books ten bucks an hour in it, in the meantime. Twelve if I made it three months.

I turned up my first day, midmorning, to be paired with Fede—an Argentine immigrant breaking in as an illustrator, when he wasn't drawing an off-the-books weekday income wandering the streets of Mt. Pleasant. He was handsome, nondescript, and all business—which he probably had to be. While he'd married an American woman, he wasn't a U.S. citizen yet, and in our conversations I got the distinct impression that every resource made available to him was quickly allocated to maintaining any and all stability in his world. He retrieved a page-length strip of paper from the "work" table near the door off the back of our boss's kitchen, broken out into four sets of four names. It should've been a sobering hint of what was to come, but the physicality of what it foreshadowed was lost on me. A corresponding ring of keys was retrieved and we set out south into the neighborhood.

After three days, I was so sore I could scarcely move during my off-hours. Every muscle ached and dragged with an unwieldy fatigue—even during more rested, energized moments. Somehow, I hadn't considered that walking nonstop for four to five hours a day was well outside anything I'd ever demanded of my body. It kicked the living shit out of me. My inner thighs chafed to the point of being open wounds, some days. My toes formed blisters as big as the toes themselves. My lips cracked and bled from the cold and exposure; my fingers followed suit from handling keys every few minutes, in the dry, open air. And then there was the rain.

Yet after three weeks, making as much if not more than I would've in any nonprofit gig for which I was qualified; struck by how little interpersonal drama came home with me each day; and beside myself at getting to spend my work hours bounded by some of the most gorgeous architecture the District had on offer, I did as my forebears ambling about Central Park had: I abandoned any and all plans to return to office life.

There was simply no compelling reason to go back. Even when committing to a more conventional work environment held the possibility of advancement, it was a gamble contingent upon pairing overperformance with the stress of groveling; one in which the house almost always won. The whole enterprise seemed rigged to induce unrewarded increases in productivity, and in the nonprofit world, this came with a loaded ration of moral weight. You were shamed into working for nothing, for the sake of "the cause." In a stunning bit of self-caricature, friends working for AFSCME as union organizers were fired for trying to unionize, themselves. I, on the other hand, just had to ride my bike, be nice to people, and hang out with dogs. It was basically every eight-year-old's dream. I slept in, waking most days at 10 a.m. Eventually, seeking to cover later walks, my boss staggered my day, starting me at 1 p.m. There was no pressure to do my work faster, more intensely, or more productively. Further, it was *finite*. When it was done, it was done. My life outside of work hours was mine.

In truth, it did take some adjustment. I had spent my then short adult life earnestly committed to certain principles, and surreptitiously bound up with that was a sense that the present was—at least in presentation—a sacrifice toward something greater. Movement-building was, for my milieu, very much akin to old-school cathedral-building; you didn't expect to see results in your lifetime. It wasn't far off from the work ethic most of us inherited from our parents or our culture more generally—it just eschewed any attention to investment those might've counseled. Our postadolescent pursuit of authenticity was all about self-denial. So the prospect of making introductions at an organizing meeting, or some social gathering, and having to say out loud that I made my living in a manner that had real *joy* at its center was embarrassing. We had, after all, lampooned the subculture of dumpster diving, scamming, and otherwise siphoning off capitalism's excess, as a lifestylist cop-out in radical clothes. Even working for a global debt-relief coalition with questionable ties to the Democrats showed more of a spine; at least the compromise there was in the name of something *not* strictly self-indulgent. Dog walking was different. It seemed childish. It flagged a shrugging resignation to the absurd consumer whims of late capitalism, while basking in a general lack of obligation.

Ultimately, I stopped caring. The solitude of my workday proved indispensable in recovering from the disaster that had been my year up to that point. Instead of moody coworkers, or passive-aggressive bosses, I gave directions or made coffee recommendations to strangers, all of them delighted I even bothered. I keyed into thirty homes a day where I was greeted by a living being unable to contain its excitement about why I was there. I paused at regular intervals, marveling at how gorgeous my city actually was. These, among so many other subtleties, began to figure as an *enormous* privilege.

The moments of deep presence in which I noticed, and said to my-self, Holy shit, guy, this is what you're actually getting paid to do, were frequent. And, to anyone else, I could say the flexibility of my schedule freed me up to support movement work most folks I knew could not take on.

I moved my books and a few other possessions into a collective house on Seventeenth Street NW, behind a Salvadoran restaurant on Mt. Pleasant's main corridor. My rent totaled less than three days' work, and my cost of living was greatly reduced by a commu-nized economy within the house. I cooked for my housemates, and attended traffic-disrupting bike protests against the recent invasion of Afghanistan.

At night, I read used books in teahouses. And I set about be-ginning again.

5

THE DRIFT

A revolutionary action within culture must aim to enlarge life, not merely to express or explain it. It must attack misery on every front. Revolution is not limited to determining the level of industrial production, or even to determining who is to be the master of such production. It must abolish not only the exploitation of humanity, but also the passions, compensations and habits that exploitation has engendered. We have to define new desires in relation to present possibilities.

So went the 1957 manifesto *Report on the Construction of Situations and on the International Situationist Tendency's Conditions of Organization and Action*—a mouthful, as well as the founding document of a revolutionary group of artists, intellectuals, and political theorists bending what was left of Dada and surrealism toward an antiauthoritarian reinterpretation of Marx. They called themselves the Situationist International. Their ideas, disseminated largely through their own journal, would eventually provide kindling for the events of May 1968 in Paris—an uprising that came within a few breaths of toppling the government of France.

Central to their critique was the manner in which day-to-day relations in society had become increasingly mediated by objects or commodities. What had emerged amid the transformations within capitalism and the rise of mass production after World War II was something the Situationists called "the society of the spectacle," in which we figure less as participants in our own lives than spectators to a world produced *for* us. Their program sought to encourage interventions against that mediation through "the construction of situations"—subversive disruptions in (then) modern forms of alienation. Contemporary prank-driven protest culture—from The Yes Men to the magazine *Adbusters* (who put out the call to occupy Wall Street in 2011)—owes a great deal to the example of the Situationists.

Especially in their early writings, the Situationists were keenly interested in architecture and urbanism, particularly the manner by which spaces are engineered to entice or produce particular behaviors—typically, *consumer* behaviors. Life in these spaces gravitates toward commercial corridors, so even if we as residents identify with, desire, or privilege other kinds of values, highly concentrated commercial interests end up shaping the spaces that make up communities. This isn't strictly a matter of inanimate, physical structures; it quietly *becomes* the logic of the immersed population, like a spell. The Situationists were eager to break that spell, countering with what they called "psychogeography"—an approach to urban landscapes that emphasized a sort of playfulness or passion not driven by the dominant or normative psychology. "[C]ities have psychogeographical contours, with constant currents, fixed points and vortexes that strongly discourage entry into or exit from certain zones," they argued.

A key Situationist tactic was the *dérive,* or the drift. In a nutshell, the tactic involved randomly wandering through urban landscapes without reference to much beyond one's own curiosity and passions. The goal was to acquaint oneself with what one's surroundings may yield when approached without reference to commercial or administrative functions. "In a *dérive* one or more persons during a certain period drop their relations, their work and leisure activities, and all their other usual motives for movement and action, and let themselves be drawn by the attractions of the terrain and the encounters they find there," argued the founding and signature voice of the Situationist International, Guy Debord, in the 1958 essay "Theory of the *Dérive.*"

The physical and psychological training central to the *dérive* was of the same general quality as meditation. By de-emphasizing the dominant narratives one was so used to seeing that they didn't even feel like narratives, whole other *versions* of cities revealed themselves. Cities, after all, have no *singular* identity, which means that there's a whole incalculable range of possible lives to be lived.

For Debord, those possible lives were a nascent threat to the alienation characteristic of postwar capitalism.

The first hour I spent hauling dogs around Mt. Pleasant with Fede, it was apparent that dog walking required an approach to walking that had never occurred to me. From one anonymous house to the next, we carved paths that seemed to have no real purpose beyond keeping each dog out for the allotted time. Eventually, I picked up on the rhythm of cycling through dogs in sets of four. Walking was organized primarily around grouping dogs by proximity, then additionally by routes sufficient to cover the time the client paid for. The combination made for a version of Debord's *dérive*, inasmuch as the engine driving our movement had no correspondence with commercial structures in the neighborhood. In fact, given the way public life concentrated along Mt. Pleasant Street, it was best to stay as far from it as possible; the accumulation of commerce was an unnecessary distraction for dogs—and there were too many things to dodge. Once I was cleared to work unaccompanied, I quickly found myself seeking out routes that both killed time and combined elements that dialed down my attention to its passing. Back alleys and their carriage houses. The path from Park Road up through the woods on the edge of the park, to Ingleside Terrace. Crossing south through the neighborhood by way of Adams Mill Road, the audible cadence of joggers in the park and the chatter of monkeys echoing out of the National Zoo. My walks, lacking any destination beyond where I began, became occasions for exploration.

I discovered that Mt. Pleasant is a sort of peculiar neighborhood for D.C. Unlike most, its borders are somewhat clear, in a manner that makes it actually *feel* distinctive. Architecturally, it's not altogether novel for the District; late-nineteenth-century and early-twentieth-century row houses cluster around its core in its eastern half. As it slopes west into the woodsy valley terrain of Rock Creek Park and the backside of the zoo, two-story World War II–era houses dominate, with the occasional apartment building wedging upward. To the same extent that residences lean into the park, the park appears to bleed east. There's a sleepy feel. Free boxes appear on sidewalks; a cloistered, communal culture abounds.

The neighborhood's northernmost point is effectively Oak Street; a short, cul-de-sacked, tree-canopied stretch useful only for accessing the residences packed along its length. Beyond Oak, separated by a wooded, eastward-jutting leg of the park sits the neighborhood of Sixteenth Street Heights—a yawning, more suburban-feeling area of the city dotted with freestanding homes, a smattering of religious spaces, and negligibly little commercial *anything*. It's notable for little more than being a corridor in and out of the Maryland suburbs.

The southern and eastern borders of Mt. Pleasant are Harvard and Sixteenth Streets NW, respectively. At the far corner of the intersection sits All Souls, a Unitarian outpost whose bell tower was once an audible feature of public life, often used to signal various city events. In December of 1859, it rang to memorialize militant antislavery insurgent John Brown on the day of his execution. It never rang again. East of Sixteenth one finds Columbia Heights, once a poor and working-class neighborhood so neglected it didn't even have a stop on the city's Metro until the end of the 1990s. (An upgrade almost certainly made to set the table for real-estate developers, circling like vultures.) The 1968 riots that erupted at the assassination of Martin Luther King Jr. torched much of Fourteenth Street NW, which runs through the center, and it was largely left that way for the next four decades.

The Columbia Heights Metro station now sits in the shadow of a massive shopping complex that boasts a Target, Best Buy, IHOP, and other chain outlets. Towering above it to the east are comparably sized luxury condominium behemoths, the ground floors home to wine shops, Starbucks, Five Guys Burgers and Fries, and other gaudy signatures of staggering, breakneck gentrification. In the course of roughly three years, the neighborhood transformed in such a way—with such skyward density—that returning residents from only five years prior would neither recognize it, nor have much luck navigating themselves out by way of visual reference points. This "revitalization" metastasized north into Petworth; home to the Peter Maurin collective house of the Catholic Worker—a national antiwar/antipoverty movement founded by Catholic anarchist Dorothy Day, as well as the highest murder rate for sex workers in the District the summer of '98. It also crept east through working-class residential blocks toward Howard University, and south beyond U Street; once known as the District's "Black Broadway." Now, mostly tapas bars saddled by high-end condos, blocks from Frederick Douglass's former home.

Meanwhile, Mt. Pleasant sat nestled in its own little world, figuring as a sort of lunar sibling to the Adams Morgan neighborhood to its south and west. Much like the neighborhoods surrounding Columbia Heights, Adams Morgan remains inaccessible by the Metro system. For a number of decades, this kept its real estate affordable, and its proximity to the gay scene in Dupont Circle made for a sort of bohemian culture. In the sixties and seventies, it was the site of marches in support of the black liberation movement. The following two decades, it was a mainstay of the District's legendary punk scene. Pioneering hardcore and straightedge outfit Minor Threat played their first show in the living room of a house on Calvert Street. YouTube videos abound of Bad Brains—the band that inspired everyone from Minor Threat to the Beastie Boys—playing Madam's Organ, on Eighteenth Street NW. House shows in the neighborhood continued well beyond 2000, even as rents rose and professionals pushed in, priced out of other, more desirable corners of the District. Eighteenth Street NW was and continues to be a somewhat unrivaled nightlife destination (though its texture and demographics have shifted), peppered with bars and food flagging disparate international geographies, while Columbia Road unfurls east toward Columbia Heights, with its own mix of commercial and residential life.

By contrast, and unlike many other neighborhoods in the northwest quadrant of the District, Mt. Pleasant wasn't much of a destination for anyone who didn't live there, and it appeared mostly unaffected by what swirled around it. Its main corridor sat at a sort

of random, awkward northwest–southeast angle in relation to the
gridded network of streets with which it intersected, and accessing
the neighborhood from the south, by car, required an unwieldy left-
then-right dogleg west by way of Sixteenth and Harvard. In short,
there was no *passing through* Mt. Pleasant. One was either coming or going. The vectors by which the unfolding gentrification of
adjacent neighborhoods might've bled in were too circuitous and
inhibiting; half of them bounded by woods. That buffer allowed for
an unlikely calm, given the location, as well as a class and ethnic
diversity unseen in most parts of the United States, to say nothing
of the District, itself.

My walks weaved past longstanding collective houses with deep
roots, held down by activists and artists. The Harvard Street House,
long an organizing base around a host of global justice movements.
The Lamont Street Collective, established in the mid-1970s by John
Acher, a mainstay of the D.C. Socialist Party, and the neighboring
house where many an activist fundraising party went down. My
own newfound home on Seventeenth Street NW, Casa del Ajo—a
collective with a tenure rivaling Lamont Street's, and the collective
house around the corner on Kilbourne, a frequent space for meetings and protest-puppet construction for the spring 2000 actions
against the IMF and World Bank, bought by a web developer who'd
managed all tech coordination involved. A stone's throw away, in a
clandestine space, Radio CPR—Mt. Pleasant's own bilingual pirate
radio station broadcasted illegally on 97.5 FM. A few blocks to the
north was Community Garden Co-op, a community-run health-

food cooperative administered democratically (and illegally) by residents for more than a quarter century. I barely knew the names of the businesses along Mt. Pleasant Street, the neighborhood's main corridor, but the grid of insurgent culture had imprinted itself on me.

More than a decade before my arrival in the neighborhood, a house on the corner of Nineteenth Street and Park Road (a block from where I first interviewed for my job), known colloquially as "The Embassy," had quietly staged enormous interventions on popular culture. Chief among them was the Nation of Ulysses, a heavily soul-influenced punk outfit that lived and rehearsed and occasionally recorded there. Their debut album *13-Point Program to Destroy America* had greeted early nineties punk rock like an IED. Song titles included "A Kid Who Tells on Another Kid is a Dead Kid," and the sound hijacked the raw sexuality of James Brown, shoving it down the throat of hypermasculine, self-serious late-eighties hardcore. The band favored dissonance and chaos punctuated by snare-heavy staccato over the metal-crossover sound gaining popularity in the hardcore scene—and pompadours and close-fitting suits over long-codified punk fashion. Everything about them was a "fuck you"; a throwback to the very disruptions proposed by the Situationists, including the curve ball thrown by their charismatic singer, Ian Svenonious, lying about his age to win the title of *Sassy* magazine's first "Sassiest Boy in America." "The reason I entered the contest is to indoctrinate youth gone astray," he told *The Washington Post*. "There are so many kids dressing like Grateful Dead people. It's kind of tedious." Explaining his selection, *Sassy* seemed to try to channel Nation of Ulysses's own tendency toward frontal assault, with awkward results. "As soon as we opened Ian Svenonius's entry to our Sassiest Boy in America Contest, we just knew," they wrote. "The way you know it's time to change your tampon."

While I shouldn't have been, I was surprised when Ian and I crossed paths just outside the neighborhood, *both* of us walking dogs. He worked for a different agency, but we frequented the same newly opened vegan bakery in Adams Morgan between walks, and our schedules somehow synced up such that we saw each other and contrived attempts at shoptalk, almost daily, for a time. By then, *Sassy* had long since discovered his ruse, and revoked his award. Even years later, one couldn't help but admiringly chuckle at the fact that he'd thought to pull such a prank, much less that he'd managed such a brilliant satirical coup in the process. And in that same historical moment, Nation of Ulysses had radically altered the contours of punk, and by extension, mainstream music; their sonic and visual aesthetics found their way as far up the food chain as MTV. Sweden's garage rock export, The Hives, who were practically impossible *not* to hear on the radio or in a commercial a full ten years after Nation of Ulysses's debut, were a naked derivation to anyone who'd heard *13-Point Plan to Destroy America*. Further, The Embassy had served as a sometimes home to folks who would go on to become Bikini Kill—the band at the eye of the storm that became the riot grrrl movement; a women-led, feminist expropriation of punk rock's liberatory potential. Early zines from the movement were rumored to have been produced in The Embassy's living room. Punk culture and feminism were never the same.

This insurgent, rebellious current within the neighborhood—particularly its punk manifestations—had roots many seemed to have forgotten. During its "Dirty War" period, refugees fleeing to the United States from El Salvador landed in a number of cities, D.C. being their second most frequent destination. Many of them settled in Mt. Pleasant. The brutal Salvadoran regime at the time was a client state of the United States, so there was no humanitarian crisis in El Salvador that the State Department was willing to acknowledge, which meant that refugee status was not on offer. Thus, the Salvadoran population concentrating in the neighborhood was largely undocumented. This had predictable results.

Extended families crammed into one- and two-bedroom apartments, frequently subjected to unannounced INS raids. Contractors would prey on the neighborhood, hiring desperate, undocumented day laborers simply for their lack of recourse to *any* legal protections—often with the promise of pay that never materialized. Cops were cops, engaging in the sorts of harassment and excessive force communities of color typically report, a pattern exacerbated by a lack of Spanish-speaking officers. Meanwhile, scant immigrant household resources were being sent home to help spring other family members from the very war the United States was actively funding. By the time the nineties rolled around, tensions were boiling.

On May 5, 1991, a rookie cop attempted to arrest a Salvadoran man for disorderly conduct following Cinco de Mayo festivities in

Adams Morgan. Somehow, the man was shot and left paralyzed. Worse, he'd been shot while handcuffed, and as news of it circulated, Mt. Pleasant exploded. Hundreds of young people took to the streets, attacking cops. Footage from the events shows running street battles, police cruisers torched, and nominal looting. The unrest intensified throughout the night, diffused only by rain as the sun rose. City negotiations with local community figures failed to bottle a second night of clashes, as did the arrival of some one thousand riot police. For a second night, hundreds of black and Latino youth fought cops in the streets. Tear gas was fired. City buses were set ablaze. Ultimately, the mayor declared a state of emergency and a 7 p.m. curfew was imposed on the neighborhood, as well as Adams Morgan and Columbia Heights. In the end, some fifty people had been reported injured—mostly cops. More than sixty police vehicles had been damaged in some fashion, some destroyed completely. In a twist quite at odds with punk politics, which often figured as little more than posturing, residents of The Embassy—in particular, members of the Nation of Ulysses—were storied participants in the uprising; fighting cops alongside their neighbors.

It was impossible for me *not* to hear these histories coming out of the walls as I looped my way through Mt. Pleasant. And it thus became a completely different place to me than what bus routes, city talking points, or "Business Improvement Districts" would have presented. Further, walking neighborhoods day in and day out meant an intimacy with my world from the bottom up. The moving parts of daily life at the ground level began to feel far more inter-

esting, textured, and vibrant than even the abstractions and aspirations that animated my downtime in organizing meetings and
social movements.

On some level, it was sobering. There is, after all, a certain re-
ligiosity and self-assuredness that binds people hunkered down on
front lines where the cadence of police beatings and the user in-
terfaces of far-flung horrors (usually United States–backed) meet.
Faced with such lopsided odds, concise narratives and priorities
dominate, and the allowances made for frivolity or joy typically
conform to some orthodoxy or another. It owes more to a dispersed,
affiliative notion of "community" than anything geographically
immediate. More "Catholic community" than regulars at a corner
café. At work, in that most days was less a tendency toward disin-
genuousness than tunnel vision. All of it was nothing if not earnest
and well intentioned. The candor and lack of predictability in my
encounters with dogs, people, places, and rhythms in my walking
day grew more fascinating, felt notably less scripted, and frankly
became easier to trust.

Nascent possible new lives, exactly as Debord had suggested.

6

SPOILER: DOGS ARE ASSHOLES

One of the first things people say when you tell them you're a dog walker is, while predictable, a bit grating in its lack of perspective: "Oh, you must love dogs!"

Here's the thing, folks: I've been vegan more than half my life. I cut my teeth as an activist by gluing the locks of fur stores. *Of course* I love dogs. I love *all* animals. Enough to build into my life a discipline that insists they're not means to my ends. Enough to have spent a number of years professionally jockeying the databases and outreach tables of animal-rights organizations for no benefits and the pay such organizations offer entry-level candidates. Enough to suffer the tunnel vision and garbage social skills of people who show up for anything animal rights related. Enough to avoid getting fired from such work by humoring a cougar-like board member of my workplace who'd cornered me at an event to make a case for some moral distinction between zoophilia and bestiality that I can now never unhear.

What you all mean is that I must *enjoy* dogs.

Yeah.

That feels weird, now that you're wondering whether that cougar-lady *enjoyed* dogs, doesn't it?

Anyway. While working with them gave me a deeper, far more candid appreciation of dogs and their personalities, the fact is that doing the job day in and day out kinda required me to enjoy dogs *less*. What we so love about dogs—what must drive at least 50 percent of YouTube's traffic—is the utter lack of fucks they give about even being *intelligible* to humans much of the time, to say nothing of their being creatures to whom our interests are generally incidental and inane. Both of these are enormous impediments to retrieving dogs from their homes; walking them grouped with other dogs they may or may not know, through a veritable obstacle course of distractions; and regimenting it all on sometimes airtight timelines. *Enjoying* the quirky novelty and lack of predictability dogs often exhibit is likely to get you fired by most agencies. Sure. In hindsight, the shit dogs do is *hilarious*, charming—even downright heart melting sometimes. But in the moment, in the field? It's an enormous pain in the ass.

And often, this put me quietly at odds with clients, their needs and expectations clashing with their illusions about their animal(s). In just about any case, a client is unlikely to be impressed that you never managed to get their sweet, fragile little baby outside because she refused to be leashed up and sprinted laps around the apartment, colliding with just about every vertical surface, while you laughed your face off instead of doing your job. And that assumes you even *have* a relationship with the client. If you work for an agency, they're going to complain to your boss, and your boss is typically 100 percent uninterested in anything but the revenue stream your labor represents.

So, to prove I'm not a just being a total dick here, in no particular order, is:

A Possible Top Ten Asshole Dog Moments of My Career

1. The dog who, upon seeing a family unloading gifts from their SUV onto the sidewalk of an adjacent house on Christmas Day, opted to piss on said gifts while neither I nor the people in question were looking.

2. The English sheepdog whose size and lack of discipline made walking him a gamble on serious injury, who so hated the fenced-in dog park (where he might've actually gotten meaningful exercise *without* blowing out one of my knees) that, upon entering on any given day, promptly took a giant shit and then stood at its center, barking incessantly, thus confirming local residents' predictions of noise and nuisance when the park was initially proposed.

3. The golden retriever who managed to outsmart a prong collar by rearing up and crossing his front paws over the leash, neutralizing the collar's coercive effect, and making me seriously ponder an impending golden retriever rebellion-turned-global-dictatorship.

4. The springer spaniel puppies that filled their crate with straight-up liquid feces one morning, leaving it to soak invisibly into the newspapers covering the crate's floor, and me calling my boss to ask if the clients were hiding a corpse.

5. The pit bull that shredded a lover's panties, discarded in haste while she joined me on a dog sit.

6. The *other* English sheepdog that—if the visual evidence was to be believed—fired diarrhea at the walls from a canon while his people were out.

7. The stick-obsessed pit bull that refused to relinquish a fallen tree branch, and proceeded to basically key every parked car for three long blocks.

8. Any dog I ever had to walk *while* the client was home, acting as though I were dragging them off to be gassed, as passersby stared in disapproving horror.

9. The basset hounds that scavenged *everything* and taunted my gag reflex at the sight of wet tissue, by hoovering up several errant wads of it after a rainstorm on trash day.

10. The golden lab that—living up to its breed's child-friendly reputation—saw a toddler take a spill in the park and promptly set about mounting the kid, in front of his mother.

7

KEYS: A USER'S MANUAL

Half of each of my days at the Ruckus training camp in 1999 was spent learning how to climb. The goal was to learn to hang banners from buildings, bridges, and the like; the methods were those of mountaineering and rock climbing. I was horrid at it. The two things I clearly recall my trainer saying to me, in plaintive exasperation, were "Why do you do everything wrong?" and "Get out of the harness. *Right now.*" The process nonetheless imbued me with a particular awareness.

A central concept in climbing is what is known as a *point of protection*—a juncture at which a climber's weight is held, to prevent plummeting to one's death (typically). This could be a knot, a carabineer, a loop or ring in a harness or mounted to a climbing surface, and so on. There are usually a series of these doing work at any moment in a climbing scenario, and each substantive movement within a climb requires one to check the entire line of them, in a very specific order. There's a deliberate, built-in redundancy to it, and I found it excruciatingly tedious. I dropped out of high school with exactly *zero* math credit, and the whole routine of checking points of protection felt cumbersome; like the FOIL method in algebra or writing out one's multiplication with addition. If I missed a point of protection, my trainer would demand I start over and check my way through the series from the beginning. Some sessions, I'd move up the rope only two or three steps, because I simply couldn't retain the order of the points of protection I was tasked with checking. The disaster against which this convoluted process allayed was apparent enough, and yet the impulse to shrug at it and lurch forward was practically irresistible. My trainer, however, thankfully enforced firm boundaries with me, effective enough to sear at least their premise onto my consciousness.

The often cacophonous, high-school janitor-worthy ensemble of keys that distinguishes professional dog walkers from everyone else ambling about with a canine is a thing of comparable critical significance. To a casual observer, it probably figures as a collection of responsibilities, represented visually. And it *is* that. But more so than any other tool that a dog walker might need, it cannot be improvised. There's a certain severity to that distinction. Your keys are either where you need them to be, or they're not. They are, simply put, the most essential among one's points of protection, and short of informing a client their companion animal has actually *died* on your watch, few things hold a megaphone to your lack of professional competence like the news you've locked yourself out of someone's house. Such incidents render your function in the client's life fully inverted; rather than enabling them to go about their workday seamlessly, you are a disruption—one for which they typically have considerably less affection than the dog they would've come home to let out in the first place. It is a scenario absolutely agonizing in its drawn-out, multistaged humiliation, and it is to be studiously avoided.

Thus, engineering key transport and storage is an extraordinarily detail-driven matter of skill and attention. A quick guide for the uninitiated might go as follows:

- You typically have two types of keys, and they should be organized as such: midday and off-time. Midday keys ought to be to clients' homes you visit at least once a week. Off-time keys are for the occasional pet-sitting gig or that client who invariably calls you last minute to squeeze onto the day's schedule. Neither should be grouped with your personal home/car/bike keys. Carrying *all* your keys *every* day is, simply put, Amateur Hour. If nothing else—even if you're meticulous in keeping tabs on your things—muggings are a thing in U.S. cities, if less frequent than popular imagination would have it. If someone snatches your bag, and all your work keys are in it, you're left with a scenario not unlike getting bad news from the STI clinic. Not only are you stuck calling *every client* you've ever had, to sheepishly inform them of your now shared misfortune, and then acquiring new keys from those that don't spook and fire you outright—you're having that conversation with clients to whom you speak less frequently, and with whom you have less of a rapport. They are *far* less likely to empathize or forgive.

Embedded in an approach any less rigorous than this one is a sort of delusional assumption of invincibility, and a failure to account for a world that is bigger than one's self—a willingness to take unnecessary risks, mostly to dispense with nominal front-end labor (or perhaps just out of ignorance that that labor even exists). And invariably, that work will be off-loaded to someone else when the unexpected toccurs. Further, it shorts the significance of human relationships in this trade. A monkey can handle the bulk of the manual labor. It's the delicate management of clients and their— quite natural—emotional inclinations that certifies your competence. Case in point: even if a client might express surprise at your separating keys by way of this taxonomy (and you'd do well to subtly *perform* that task in front of them during any initial consultation, to seed this curiosity), the opportunity it affords to display foresight and innovation here covers considerable distance in demonstrating they've hired someone smarter than the average bear. *Be that smarter bear.* Always.

- Your keys should have two to three homes, tops. By that, I mean that they should either be *on* you, hanging from a hook on your wall, or in your bag. Period. End of story. They should not be on the end table next to your couch, on the kitchen counter, in the car of whomever you're sleeping with, on the table at the bar when you're drinking with your friends, or anywhere else. At all. Ever. In fact, fuck your bag. Don't put your keys in your bag. It's too mobile. People tend to set bags down, and I've lost count of how many walkers I know who've left a bag in a client's house while doing walks, not realizing that they'd shoved their keys back in it before leashing up the dogs and proceeding to lock themselves out. We'll leave alone entirely those who've left their bags in cafés, dressing rooms, on buses, and god knows where else. As a bonus, jagged metal has a tendency to wear holes in the materials from which bags are usually made, which is a recipe for absolute disaster. Just don't do it.

- While we're at it, this is true of your phone, as well. It should be in your pocket, or on its charger. Nowhere else. In other words, if you're working, it should be on your person—*no exceptions*. Again: *You are not omnipotent*. Don't get comfortable. I used to pass a woman on my Capitol Hill route walking a German shepherd around the neighborhood off leash (note: I'm pretty sure Hitler walked his dog off leash), as she casually read a book. Like the world was her castle courtyard. Such oblivious, lunatic people abound. (You can often find them behind the wheel of a car.) Should some emergency situation arise, and you don't have your phone, you deserve every misfortune that befalls you. I was once tasked with dispatching a coworker's client to his own home, forced to Google him from my phone and be redirected via his *former* workplace (the only Google hit I could find), after his walker had locked herself out of his building. *With his dogs.* And other dogs. *Without* her phone.

"No, you can't call her to give her the building access code."

"Why not?"

"Well . . ."

You'd think such situations comically implausible in an allegedly professional sphere. And you would be very, very wrong.

- Never, *ever* be that monster that puts clients' identifying info on key tabs. Seriously. The only things that should appear on these are the dog's name, and *your* phone number. Even pet-care agency owners fuck up on this one, inexplicably. A friend in the business once told me of a coworker who'd driven off with his work keys on the roof of his car. Every one of which had its corresponding address attached to it. They were, of course, never seen again. Aside from the obvious liability of some ne'er-do-well tracking a key to a client's home and relieving them of their possessions (or worse), ensuring a Good

Samaritan contacts *you*, rather than your client, saves you considerable face.

- Before you close any door behind you, make visual contact—not only with your keys generally, but with the very key(s) you need to get back into *that door*. If you don't see the key(s) in question, *do not close that door.* This is not merely tepid recommendation. It is an essential practice; the visual confirmation of points of protection prior to an irrevocable change of position. Generally speaking, life is a less complicated enterprise when afforded such deliberate pauses for reflection, even in the most mundane acts. Monumental stupidity and hubris lurk in the impulse to shrug out "It's cool, I've got this." No. You don't. None of us do. You are the sum of your practices and your resistance to habitual inertia. Everything else is inherited, and requires interrogation—lest you find yourself confined to the options one enjoys on the wrong side of a locked door.

- Hand-carrying such a massive, jagged wad of metal through a workday is prohibitive, and if the bottom half of your day-to-day getup is baggy enough for your pockets to prove accommodating to the task . . . well, you probably have a bit of soul-searching to do.

  The most common method for carrying work keys is a clip of some sort. But people tend to choose the worst options, here. Spring-loaded *anything* is a terrible idea in any item that gets heavy use, for the simple fact that springs eventually give out. Those key-clips popular with hipsters, bike messengers, and their ilk? They're garbage. Just don't. The enclosing mechanism that secures them is worthless once that spring goes. Plus, belt loops aren't designed to carry that kind of weight, or *any* weight, really. Blow one out, and you've basically ruined your jeans. Carabineers are a comparably popular remedy, but pose the same hazard of ripping belt loops, with the additional risk of closing *onto* the fabric of the loop, rather than *around* it—rendering the device as functional as the aforementioned clip, with a blown spring. Ask around and you're bound to find someone who lost a whole ring, for this very reason.

- After much trial and error, I decided that the most optimal methods of transporting keys were those with the fewest moving parts—the fewest *parts*, even. Moving or otherwise. Your average hardware store carries a solid metal clip that slips over and hugs the belt itself—a far more sturdy resting surface—with a tensioned closure for the key ring, not unlike a safety pin. No hinges, no springs, and better still—the entire device is one contiguous piece of metal. Keep it simple, kids. You'll be glad you did.

- Whenever possible, make backup copies. Don't ask the client; just make them. Have a backup ring with a copy of *every* key on it, and keep it somewhere accessible to your work route. Real-estate agents keep keys to properties they're showing in lockable key boxes attached to porch railings and the like, often opened by combination. If your ring is small enough to fit, find a coffee house or some other friendly business nearby where you can lock a key box in a not-obvious spot. If your ring is too big, make friends with the staff at a business nearby, and leave your spare ring behind the counter. Yes, you'll be handing your clients' keys off to little more than strangers. But provided you're not an oblivious dickhole and haven't put any clients' info on the keys, they're useless to anyone but you. If you find yourself without your keys or only a single key, you'll be thankful replacement didn't require trekking home. And your clients will be grateful they hired such a reliable, consistent, and punctual dog walker—all the while blissfully ignorant of the long-arc lateral save you've just orchestrated, behind the scenes.

8

KEYS: A TEMPLE TO GOLDILOCKS

When I returned to the United States at eighteen, I took a job at a one-hour photo lab in the Bel Air Mall, in the northern suburbs of Baltimore. The workspace looked out onto a corridor that dead ended at the food court a few yards down, and our photo printer was oriented such that prints rolled out just inches from the glass wall at the front of the shop, so waiting customers could watch from outside as their memories spilled forth for everyone to see. Why this struck anyone as a good idea, or anything but an invasion of privacy, I'll never know.

Under certain conditions, to obscure the production process, a one-foot roll of industrial-brown paper towels was affixed by its end to the top of the printer and rolled down along the conveyer. One such instance was when the Harford County Sheriff's Office would drop off its forensics photos for developing. Usually autopsy images of a woman beaten to death by an enraged partner, or some teenager attacked in the woods on a shortcut home from a weekend

party, left to die of exposure, limbs and clothing in telltale arrangements. In every case, I'm sure the outsourcing was illegal. It was
certainly an obscene violation of the victims and their families, and
I resented being made accomplice to it. When the boss wasn't there
to ensure I rang up the cops under their corporate account, I would
conveniently "forget" to give them their 50 percent discount, in
retaliation.

If, prior to the proliferation of digital photography, you ever
took nude photos or opted to document yours or your friends' sex
lives in stills, you can sleep soundly knowing that the guys and gals
working at the photo lab made their own copies. They probably
made copies for their friends, too. I know, because I more than once
returned from lunch to find the paper-towel-privacy-curtain up,
and a stack of images I wish I'd never seen thoughtfully set aside for
me by my coworkers. I didn't have to ask. They were a giving bunch.

With rare exception, anyone who's hired a dog walker has re-
linquished control of a house key, much in the same way naïve, amateur pornographers did with their film in the mid-nineties. And
a similar sort of tacit relation was constructed in that exchange,
whether all parties knew it, or not. A dog walker's key ring is, in
a very real sense, a map of a surreptitious commons, one of which
we are generally *far* more aware than clients are. Which is not to
say it's all sordid, or anything other than generally uncontroversial
and common sense. Your dog walker is probably going to use your
bathroom, for example, rather than risking everything that can go
wrong with defecating in public. And he or she might, on occasion,

pour themselves a glass of water. I'm not breaking any big news by disclosing this. Most client consultations involve an invitation to do such things.

Then, there are *other* scenarios, where mere access stands in for permission, inasmuch as no real harm is done; scenarios in which any objection is keenly unlikely. For instance, charging a phone or a laptop at a client's home. For the client, the decision to let an outsider into a private space is likely bound up with the dog walker's status as a sort of surrogate; we're performing in their stead, and thus the contours of license become blurred a bit. That surrogacy also has a temporality to it—a beginning and an endpoint. That is, there's a specific *occasion* that makes for that exception. *When you're here to walk the dog . . .* etc. But that occasion can be moved, quite literally, on a moment's notice. A last-minute work obligation requires them to schedule an evening walk, or stagger the midday visit to a later hour. So, there's nothing about the particular time of day that makes such license more or less acceptable. The operative exception is that the client is simply not home to be impacted in any way.

This is where I *am*, perhaps, revealing something of a trade secret. In some technical sense, it can be argued that my taking a piss in a client's hallway bathroom when I'm there to pick up or drop off their dog is distinct from my doing so for the simple fact that it's there, I have keys, and they're not home to care. But in the effects, and for the average dog walker, these two scenarios are identical. After all, dog walkers typically circulate in an area at once compact and familiar, so the spaces that key ring represents become less compartmentalized. One's route is simply a network of facilities at one's disposal, within the workday window.

I should be clear: I'm not talking about anything done with malice or anything even approaching malice. A dog walker who steals objects from clients' homes, for instance, is a piece of shit and has no business holding keys. But let's say I was soaked to the bone only halfway through my day, from working in the rain, and splattered with the mud and grit that any activity in such conditions entails. You can bet your *ass* that—time permitting—I might've made use of clients' showers, and thrown my clothes in their dryer. Again, the consequential dimension of such an act was whether it affected the client in any noticeable way. I'm reasonably certain most clients would not have cared, or would've at least been embarrassed to object. As their surrogate, in conditions they were perfectly happy to avoid, I'd have likely been afforded every comfort or convenience they themselves would've seized. At worst, it's presumptuous. But uncontroversial, in principle.

Here again, however, we run up against the quality of the operative exception. Let's say I also routinely spared myself the cost and hassle of Laundromats by throwing my dirty clothes in a messenger bag, and running them through both the wash and dry cycles at a client's home, checking in on things throughout the day, and retrieving it all at the end of my route. Or that I might've made a habit of taking ingredients to work with me, with which I made myself meals at clients' homes—sometimes out of timeliness; sometimes because they had a better stove or cookware than I did. Hypothetically, I could've taken naps on clients' couches when ill or fatigued, watched European football on their cable, or masturbated in their bathrooms when bored during down time between walks. It's perfectly plausible that I invited friends lacking midday obligations to join me in availing ourselves of a client's hot tub, while congressional staff shuffled past the privacy fence, back to their offices. Lacking sufficient seating in my own home, I may have scheduled and hosted reading groups in a client's residence while they were at work. It's not out of the question that, realizing I had a particularly light workday, I invited the one night stand in whose bed I'd woken up to tag along for the sheer challenge and adventure of having sex in every house on my route. And let's say that, in the course of *years* no one ever noticed. Would it matter?

I can say with some confidence that, in the actuality of how things go down, it doesn't. Likely some quantum physics angle says these things *don't* occur for the people who don't know about them. But based on my own informal surveys of colleagues in the industry, I'd bet dollars to doughnuts that all of the above—and probably much worse—happens with reasonable frequency. Including the one-night stand ride along. The rate at which clients discover such things and fire their walkers merely reflects the amateurish lack of tact certain folks bring to the routine.

9

A NOTE ON PRIVILEGE

The trust a client exercises in handing off keys to a dog walker is worthy of a sociology dissertation, especially because it was, in my experience, often a pretty lazy, cavalier affair. Rarely did prospective clients ask for references, though I had a note on my iPhone from which reference contact info could be copied and texted to a client, before I'd even shown up for the consultation. It was enough that I was nominally charming, the same way people inexplicably ask the stranger sitting next to them at the café to watch their laptop while they hit the bathroom.

Fact:

That trust is highly mediated by race and class. It was enough that I was sufficiently charming *and* white *and* articulate in ways that made people feel safe. The things I got away with doing in people's homes are ten times more shocking, given that black folks are shot on sight for knocking on a door for help after a car accident. No congressional staffer ever asked if I was legal to work in the United

States, despite the fact that revelations on that issue tanked careers in their world, routinely. I was never subjected to a background check. No anxiety was ever provoked by my spoken accent. And so on. At the end of the day, everything I did in the job and every opportunity or freedom it afforded me was an effect of race and class privilege.

While dog walking is not an *exclusively* white trade, it is nonetheless overwhelmingly so. Walk through any city where the trade operates, and you can't help but notice. Not only should the gatekeeping mechanics that account for that tell us unflattering truths about ourselves, as a culture, but it also ought to bring into focus what dog walkers outside of the trade's dominant demographics manage, on a moment-to-moment basis.

Late in my career, a particularly incompetent colleague erroneously concluded he'd *lost* a dog he was sitting for a period of days (the dog had merely hid under a bed), and having explained this to the client, panic ensued and police were called. When they arrived, he had no ID on him and could not tell the officers the clients' full names. He *may* have also been high. He was, however, definitely *white*. So none of it stopped the cops from helping him find the dog.

I'd prefer not to ponder how it'd have ended had he been black.

10

THAT QUESTION YOU'RE DYING TO ASK

Yes. Dog walkers deal with shit. *Actual* shit. Dog shit.

For some reason, this preoccupies everyone but the dog walkers doing it. And that lack of squeamishness isn't terribly interesting or profound. Go outside, and pick up the newspaper from in front of your house. If you don't get the paper, steal your neighbor's. Slide that plastic bag-sheath thing off of it. Put your hand in that bag, like it's one of those oversized rubber gloves your mom wore to wash dishes. Now pick up any object outside, using that hand—a rock, some leaves, whatever. It doesn't matter. Peel the bag off your hand, turning it inside out, so that whatever object you've picked up is concealed in it. *The end*.

How long did that take you? About five seconds. A dog-walking route one could rank at the high side of average would involve doing this roughly thirty times. Two-and-a-half minutes. In four hours. I could rattle off any number of things in a dog walker's workday that take up more time than that, and certainly take up more mental energy.

Common rectal hygiene in much of the world involves considerably more direct hand-to-shit contact than dog walking. And it's probably instructive in more ways than I can address in this short work that, as an American, the overwhelming majority of people who dilettantishly ask me if I'm squeamish about dog excrement are—unlike, say, much of the Muslim world—passing their tidy days with a mix of toilet paper and shit smeared up their ass cracks. Freedom isn't free, I guess.

I have three major problems with the premise of poop anxiety. First, the apocalypse we seem to think will swallow us whole if our taboos around bodily fluids and functions are transgressed is horseshit. Let me assure you, if you live in a city, pretty much every outdoor surface below knee height is covered in piss. You literally *live* in a piss-soaked environment. Dogs have taken care of that for you. Thankfully, in most cities outside California and the southwestern United States, it rains from time to time, and the piss-index dips for a day or two. So there's a periodic reprieve. Nonetheless, this bizarre, sanitized construction of life that we so fiercely defend from contamination is little more than a story we tell ourselves. And it's dumb. The vast majority of the world is not nearly so tidy, and people manage to not only survive, but accomplish feats that defy the imagination. Welcome to the grown-up table.

Second, *babies*. Seriously. Most of you are procreating like mad, which means you're handling quantities and varieties of shit that ought to induce nightmares, and not infrequently taking a stream of piss to the face in the process. Worse, you're willingly sleep deprived (and have very likely forfeited all greater life aspirations) for the privilege. Even once you've graduated that phase of parenthood, you're going to be wiping the equivalent of a very drunk person's shitty asshole for another few years. And you're seemingly incapable of shutting up about how it's the greatest thing ever.

Third, I am deeply skeptical of universal truth-claims of any stripe. But there is *one* truth I regard as absolute and unchanging, and it is that poop = funny. In fact, I am positively *evangelical* about this fact. If you don't think bodily functions are absolutely hilarious, I'm not sure I even want to talk to you. And walking dogs for a living really only dialed in my devotion on that score. When a dog locks eyes with you while backing out a grumpy, with that mixture of spite and deep confusion in their expression—that is an incredibly special moment. The fact that you live in world where that even happens ought to make you want to go door to door with The Good News. When someone shits their pants—it doesn't even matter if the cause happens to be life threatening. With time, it's *still* funny. When one dog moves in to sniff something another has decided to mark, and you wind up taking him home with piss on his face? Incredible. When one dog locks in to pinch a few off and in his delicately balanced and highly vulnerable position gets his face fucked by an eager peer nearby? Day maker.

This is a dog walker's *job*. To bear witness to the most powerful truth on offer, and bask in it. 'Tis no burden, friend.

11

MOSES

"At the time, I weighed just over one hundred pounds." Cody was a slight—if indomitably scrappy—young woman when I met her. She once witnessed an accident while working, and pinned a guy twice her size to his car by his collar after hearing him hurl racist slurs at the cabbie he'd struck.

"Just to put things into perspective, this dog had ten pounds on me."

We'd worked together in D.C., where she fronted a rather heavy, experimental punk band that acquired quite a profile in its short tenure. She also had virtually no filter when it came to conversation. I was as liable to hear of her one-night stand with a renowned anarcho-primitivist* and how she punted him out of bed for boycotting oral sex with women who forewent shaving as I was to learn how many days she could go without showering before

_____

* A wing-nut denomination of anarchist hostile to technology, civilization, and (in some cases) even language.

her crotch "smelled like a hamster cage." Both of these topics were as unremarkable—and as likely to be fodder for discussion—as an account of what she had for breakfast. It's not that she was particularly bawdy, or sought to provoke out of some need for attention. Quite the opposite. She was unpretentious almost to a fault. Mostly, she just lacked much of a threshold for bullshit. And hangups and modesty were, in her estimation, bullshit. They were methods by which people set themselves apart, or exempted themselves from the messiness and complexity of everyone else's lives. And she lived that sentiment intuitively, without a whiff of apology.

Having since become a yoga instructor in Los Angeles, Cody was considerably more physically sturdy sitting across from me over brunch in Silver Lake. "I don't know what breed he was—a black lab mixed with something *huge*. All I know is he looked really menacing, and his name was Moses—a commanding moniker that, I guess, kinda suited him." Our waitress gently dropped our menus on the table in passing, clearly trying to not to disrupt our conversation. Formidable presentation notwithstanding, Moses was apparently a sweet dog. He possessed an energy that, combined with his sheer body mass, made him a bit of a wild card. But neither made for actual aggression. He was walked in tandem with a neighbor's dog, in the U Street area, a few blocks east of where I'd first met Dougie.

"I think that dog"—the neighbor's dog—"was a *chuggle*," Cody speculated, yanking her menu down abruptly, not sure if the term even existed. "A pug . . . mixed with a *chihuahua, I guess?* I think it's actually called a *chug*." There is apparently no end to the branding devised to distinguish hybrid breeds of dogs, themselves bred to mitigate the absolute catastrophe that is pure breeding—while, of course, retaining an elite distinction of some variety. These designer mixes will, no doubt, be further bred for their specific characteristics, recreating the same abusive shit-show that a lack of genetic diversity has already handed these poor animals. We ordered coffee, and the waitress made her way back toward the kitchen.

"His name was Darby, and since his legs were so much shorter, walking them together meant Moses was constantly ahead of me, pulling, while Darby lagged behind, creating a split-arm thing, for me." This particular piece of information was important, hinting at a methodological nuance potentially crucial to the story's trajectory. Popular depictions of dog walkers typically feature a sole walker surrounded by umpteen dogs, leashes grouped on each arm. It's not clear from whence this image came, but much of what it conveys is nonstandard. Walkers in Buenos Aires are reputed to work up to twenty dogs simultaneously, though I never witnessed it myself during my time there. Granted, I visited within a year of the 2001 financial collapse. The middle class had been gutted by the debt default, and the rich had largely fled (or at least their money had). So it's not clear whose dogs anyone would've been walking, professionally. Either way, it's been observed, and is held up as an extreme instance of this caricature.

There's also a network of Brazilians rumored to be pack-walking as many as sixteen dogs at a time on Manhattan's Upper East Side.

As one dog walker in the neighborhood explained it, they work in volume, charging something like 60 percent of market rate. So a single dog brings in fifty dollars a week or so. To break into the field, a new walker "buys" clients for a few hundred dollars, working off the cost of the investment (for roughly two months) from more veteran walkers in the network, whose foothold and rapport generate new business.

Beyond these two scenarios, I've found it uncommon to see anyone walking more than six dogs at once, and any group over four is a red flag for lousy judgment. Dogs don't like being crowded. It makes them anxious. You're not providing any meaningful service if the end result is an aggravated, stressed-out companion animal. Additionally, crowding can yield disaster in unanticipated situations. Without even the provocation of a pack walk, two Welsh terriers with fierce leash-aggression once turned on *each other*, set off by the mere sight of another dog on our walk. As I attempted to separate them, they attacked my pant legs, shredding the lower half of a pair of jeans. (I promptly carted them home, and shitcanned the client.)

The matter of method in question is this: in my experience, even with a full group of four, all dogs are best leashed to the same arm, so as to keep a hand free for managing other things—namely *emergencies*. Your hand should be put fully *through* the loops at the end of the leashes, grasping where the lead and the loop meet. This tightens the loops around the hand so that if a dog pulls, the force is against the upside of where your hand meets your wrist, providing a second point of protection to the force of your actual grasp. This configuration also allows you to quickly shorten the lead by winding it around your fist with a simple wrist rotation. All the while, your other hand remains free.

Some will argue this is a matter of preference or style, and I would have to respectfully disagree. Even in the case of two dogs that walk at differing paces, or who tend to wind each other up and thus need to be separated a bit, your free hand can grasp one lead farther down, make a loop around that fist with a single rotation, and allow you to utilize *both* hands in the management of the dogs, with the same effect of leashing dogs to separate arms. Should some contingency arise (as is inevitable), that hand can be freed up by simply releasing the lead already anchored to the other hand, and everyone is still secure.

"Moses had a high prey drive," Cody lamented, over the lip of a coffee mug. For the layperson, such a term may require some unpacking. A veterinarian or animal behaviorist would likely give some more sophisticated explanation, but the most important bit for a dog walker is: indoors, only a *squirrel* is a squirrel; outdoors, *everything* is a squirrel. It's not like this was news to Cody. She'd been in the game a few years. "Dogs chase squirrels. Moses wanted to chase squirrels." Our waitress refilled our coffee and took our orders.

One stretch of their typical walk ran along a picket fence that turned at the adjacent property's line. The divide was in the middle of the block; the picket fence cornered and continued back along

the property line between the grassy edge of one plot and an apartment building. Between the picket fence and the wrought-iron fence
around the apartment building, there was a gap of about a foot and
a half. "Darby was, of course, lagging behind me. I think I had just
checked the time on my BlackBerry, and was looking back at him
as I put it back in my pocket." Hungover hipsters had taken up at
the table next to ours, and were browsing menus. They'd eyed us on
their way in, but had otherwise ignored us.

It'd be easy to read some fault into Cody's admitted distraction,
but the truth is that such multitasking is part of the job. Take a dog
home too early, and the time-stamped text message a client receives
from their home security system can leave you with a lot of pointless
explaining. And anyway, there are certain unavoidable calamities
that necessarily come with tethering oneself to an impulsive breed
of mammal endowed with sensory capacities well out of proportion
with its intelligence. Sometimes, you simply aren't equipped to pre-
empt. Blown knees, fractured heels, and occasional road rash are
inevitable, and put other potential downsides into perspective. You
learn to live with the lesser defeats. "If it goes *squish*, be happy it's
not a chicken bone," one coworker was fond of saying with regard
to dogs prone to scavenging. "If it goes *crunch*, be happy it's not a
condom."

And it's largely down to this that Cody didn't stand a chance on
this particular day. Moses darted abruptly to the right, lunging into
the gap between the two properties, with enough force to pin her to
the picket fence. Everything around her stopped. Her senses jolted

into self-preservation. The force of Moses pulling was quartering her on the pickets. "All I could think was *What the everloving fuck is he doing?*" Bracing her back against the fence, she leveraged her full weight to pull him back out onto the sidewalk, wagering some harm to the dog over further injury to herself. Her efforts broke the momentum enough to regain her footing and drag the dog back out into view. There was a momentary relief in having forced the scenario back into the general vicinity of standard operating procedure.

It took a few seconds for her to fully take in what she was looking at. "And then it hit me. Like, straight up took the air from my lungs. *He had a cat in his mouth.*" I heard a spoon hit ceramic, and the table to my left fell silent. It wasn't altogether clear whether the cat was a stray or the resident of some neighboring household. It didn't altogether *matter*, at that point. What did matter was that she and Moses were officially living in two different worlds. One, a horror show. The other, a triumph. Amid the carnage and piercing, agonized howls he'd instigated, Moses was absolutely *beaming*.

Terrified by Cody's panic and likely anticipating some expression of food-aggression from Moses, Darby was pulling relentlessly, scrambling in the other direction with what must've been an adorable desperation, panicked paws sputtering, practically carving evidence of the whole ordeal into the sidewalk. Seizing Moses by the collar with one hand, Cody looped the smaller dog's leash onto the fence with the other and turned to the unfolding torture scene. "Not knowing what else to do, I reached inside Moses's mouth, and

of course he just clenched his jaws around the cat, even tighter."
Our waitress stopped in her tracks, close enough for me to see her
eyes widen in a sideways glance. A crowd of onlookers was forming
off U Street. Tears poured forth, mostly from adrenaline, as Cody
pried Moses's jaws apart. The insistence with which he was seizing
his prey had cut wounds into her hands, and she began visualiz-
ing the unknowns of the stray cat's blood, comingling with hers.
"I thought, Great, now I've got hepatitis." I could practically *hear*
every head within earshot spin in our direction. It was as though
I had an app on my phone, randomly generating unsettling non
sequiturs.

Then, as if on cue, she took it to eleven: "I don't know if it was
like what you hear about happening in executions, or if Moses had
just punctured the cat's bowels, but I was suddenly covered in shit."
The hipsters closed their menus.

She couldn't remember how, but she managed to free the cat from
Moses's jaws. "But it was totally mangled and all kinds of fucked up;
hobbling and howling." Cody had a cat, herself, and was a devotee
of the species. Few things could've been more visually traumatiz-
ing. Her sobbing took on a second wave—this time out of the sheer
irrevocability of what was transpiring. Suddenly, as if mounting a
"fuck you" to her shock and sadness, the cat—still not quite dead—
started hissing, stumbling over itself, charging back at Moses, pro-
voking him. "I was in awe. Like, *how fucking stupid could this cat
be?*" Without warning, Moses struck, snatching it back into his jaws.
The number of onlookers spiked with the sudden re-escalation.

People were jumping out of their cars. One inexplicably leapt out brandishing a bat, threatening to beat Moses, if Cody didn't kick him. "I didn't want *him* intervening. So I did it." The blow was clumsy and ineffectual. Moses startled, but his prey was not dislodged. Such a blunt gesture could scarcely do more than compound an already obscene comedy. "I still feel bad about it. I mean, I straight up kicked that dog in the face." Chairs could now be heard, scooting away from us.

For no particular reason, without prompting, Moses released the cat. As if he'd simply lost interest, oblivious to the carnage and exasperation he'd foisted onto the world. Shaking, sobbing, Cody pulled out her BlackBerry to dial animal control. The cat had pulled itself behind a fire hydrant, writhing and wailing in the background. "I looked up D.C. animal control's number, and as I was doing it, I could see I was pressing blood and actual shit into my BlackBerry's keyboard." Two tables in our vicinity promptly emptied, without warning. Our waitress was visibly annoyed. Looking up into the street as she listened to the ringing on the other end of the line, Cody could see the size of her audience, and snapped into a sort of self-awareness. "I was *covered* in blood, shit, and tears. So was my phone. And I was pressing it into my ear. Everyone watching must've wanted to ask me out." Wiping her nose with her sleeve, she let the state of her wretched spectacle sink in. A full day of walks remained. As animal control took their time in arriving, the cat passed unceremoniously, in likely and rather senseless agony. The crowd dispersed. Moses and Darby were returned to their homes.

Every adjacent table was now emptying, as Cody explained that the people who'd hired her to walk Moses seemed more suspicious about how he got ahold of a cat than they were concerned with her well-being, physical or otherwise. Cody biked back up Meridian Hill to her next set of clients, a few minutes behind schedule.

And we finished brunch, as if our conversation had been completely normal.

12

MOVING TARGETS

When Pierre L'Enfant designed D.C., a central feature of his task was making the city difficult to invade. It's legendary for confounding tourists and newcomers alike, despite not being meaningfully any more complicated than Manhattan. The city's laid out on what is in effect a modified grid, with diagonal corridors cutting through it, forming sharply angled intersections at various points, with the District's signature circular nodes scattered throughout. Viewed from above, or with experience, it's fairly intuitive and navigable. At street level, it can feel like a maze.

In the fall of 2002, L'Enfant's plan was given a modern-day test-drive, when John Allen Muhammad, a veteran of the first Gulf War, and Lee Boyd Malvo, his stepson, carried out a three-week, slow-motion rampage of random sniper shootings across the metro D.C. area. By the time they were taken into custody, they'd killed ten people. In the thick of it, as the shock of each successive shooting escalated local panic, surprisingly few leads emerged. A white delivery van here. Some other description elsewhere. It was as though the shooter were simply dissolving into the surroundings, the local population hunted by a ghost. In the end, it was a fairly nondescript sedan, from which random people were picked off with a Bushmaster XM-15 rifle, at considerable distance. Usually, within a stone's throw of a highway on-ramp, or some major state route.

Only *one* of the murders occurred inside the District, and—at that—only a few blocks across the border from Maryland, on a major north–south artery. The city's design seemed to retain the protective function L'Enfant had hoped it would, even in reverse. The shooters appeared to have concluded they couldn't have easily staged an attack deep within its borders *and* had recourse to an efficient escape route. Maryland and Virginia suffered the brunt of the death toll, as a result. Bodies stilled or bleeding out in strip-mall parking lots, or outside gas stations.

Of course, this was just over a year after the September 11 attack on the Pentagon, and as things were unfolding, no one knew where the next shooting would occur. So, even as it became apparent the killings were largely a suburban phenomenon, paranoia gripped the District. Schools stopped having outdoor recess. People stopped filling up their gas tanks, for fear of what might happen if anyone stood still too long. Offices allowed employees to work from home. Commercial rhythms dropped off abruptly; no one wanted to walk to the store, or the café, or anywhere that would leave them exposed. Everywhere, people seemed visibly shaken. And everywhere, extraordinary shifts occurred to absorb and accommodate that terror.

As with most such threats, the way it was discussed sat some distance from the way it played out in the real world. Most white Americans—despite an existential foundation in and continued enthusiasm for breathtaking acts of violence—are mostly oblivious as to what life looks or feels like when it's acted on by any force greater than themselves. We're content to mine our own imaginations, assured of our own special circumstances, at a safe distance from anyone with direct experience—whose accounts are often so recurrent that they blur into white noise. For many places in the world, anguish, humiliation, and memory all mostly figure as dull aches woven into whatever new normal violence produces. With little other choice, lives go on. People fall in love. Children are born. Art is made. Poetry is written. *Somehow.* During the very dates in question, the Israeli human-rights group B'Tselem recorded more than twice as many Palestinian civilians killed by Israeli snipers, while mothers gave birth in cars and elders died of heart attacks waiting to pass checkpoints; all financed and diplomatically insulated by staggering sums in U.S. aid. As Muhammed and Malvo stalked the metro D.C. region, the United States was a full year into occupying Afghanistan, deputizing warlords and narco-traffickers, when its own soldiers weren't gunning down civilians. Within six months, it would illegally invade and occupy Iraq. And eventually, we'd all be invited to empathize with one of its most fundamentalist and *lethal* zealots, in a film that could've just as likely immortalized the Beltway shootings: *American Sniper*. The fulcrum on which such terms toggle between terrifying and heroifying suggests a hierarchy of intelligibility in the domains of fear, suffering, and bodily harm. Some fear is more real than others. Even when it's not.

Meanwhile, I was walking dogs.

Out in the open. Four to five hours a day, in broad daylight.

Perhaps more significantly, I was often spitting distance from an entrance to the Rock Creek Parkway, Connecticut Avenue, or Sixteenth Street—all major northbound corridors to the Beltway. My boss gave us permission to shorten walks to reduce exposure, if we felt unsafe, as though the routine of our movements wouldn't have made us as easy to case, regardless. Some of the clients were just staying home from work—and I was *still* being paid to show up at their homes, to spare them going outdoors any more than was absolutely necessary. I watched whole neighborhoods go very nearly silent, practically reduced to ghost towns.

I didn't resent the expectation that I continue working, inasmuch as I didn't feel altogether threatened. Autumn in the District is bested only by spring, and I honestly kind of relished the bizarre and unlikely sort of privacy I'd suddenly acquired. What *did* seem strange was the standard of danger or threat applied in the whole story, which itself seemed to prop up a delusional construction of urban life.

To hear other dog walkers tell it—and I'm speaking, here, of women and transgender dog walkers—walking the District *never* felt safe. It was (and remains) a gauntlet of unwanted interactions, catcalls, stalking, and threats of everything from rape to murder. Ask any not-male dog walker how many shitty interactions they've had with men *that day*, and you're likely to hear *harrowing* stories. Simply doing their job requires walking into the lion's den of patriarchal social relations; a nonnegotiable hours-long daily immersion in men's entitlement to their bodies, their attention, and their sexuality. The quiet war to which women are subjected broadly, is magnified, intensified, and situated as an occupational hazard.

According to a two-thousand-person international study commissioned by Stop Street Harassment and conducted by the surveying firm GfK, 65 percent of women surveyed experienced street harassment. Of that percentage, at least 70 percent reported harassment ranging from honking and leering from passing cars, to whistling and kissing noises, to sexist and sexually explicit comments, to vulgar gestures. Smaller—but nonetheless sizable—percentages reported their path being blocked by a stranger, or being the target of public masturbation. Twenty percent of women surveyed had been followed by someone on the street. Twenty-three percent had been sexually touched or groped in some way. Nine percent had been forced into some sexual act. It warrants repeating that these are the realities of women going about normal daily routines. Going to work. Getting coffee. Running errands. Exercising. Using taxis. Riding public transit. Fetching their kids from school or daycare. It amounts to, in every meaningful way, a psychic *siege*. Factor in that it's a dog walker's *job* to be walking that world, exposed, the better part of the working day, and the landscape quickly comes into terrifying focus.

You'd think the presence of a dog, or especially a pack of dogs, would be a deterrent. And you'd be wrong. Browse community forums, Google relevant search terms—and you quickly find myriad accounts of women walking their *own* dogs navigating unwelcome behavior from men, and the often elaborate routines women undertake to minimize the very real risks that come with it. For dog walkers, there's the added vulnerability of moving in and out of *enclosed* spaces. Keying into a (male) client's apartment, to then find them home unexpectedly, has a completely different set of risks for women—to say nothing of any recourse a walker would have were a client to engage in unwelcome behavior. What pet-care agency is going to take a hit to revenue (both real, and potential—existing clients always represent a referral vector), or risk potential litigation from well-resourced clients, when they can simply replace a walker with whom there's been "a problem"?

Predictably, I've never *once* heard the issue of street harassment or the threat of violence embedded within it mentioned by the pet-care industry, despite that the very service upon which they're premised *forces* a significant number of people to live in a sort of increased exposure, like bartenders before indoor smoking bans. This goes for the two major professional associations that represent the pet-care industry, as well as outfits where I was employed. No partnering with anti–street harassment organizations. No explicit allowances or policy for shortening walks in the face of harassment or threatening behavior. No assurance that the workplace will go to bat for someone in cases where that would prove useful. Not even the offer of funded self-defense classes. The fact that this collective shrug strikes anyone in the industry as even *defensible* is absolutely galling. It reflects a frankly shocking disregard for the lives and well-being of real people; perhaps a microcosm of the callousness with which the issue is treated more broadly.

Even just a moment's reflection on the numbers ought to provoke a deep and visceral shame, if not blood-boiling rage: in the fall of 2002, public life in and around D.C. ground to a slow ebb because ten people in a population of roughly three million were killed by a team of fringe sociopaths. Both the victims and the perpetrators represented negligible *fractions* of a percentage of the sample population. Comparatively, the percentage of women reporting being physically violated by strangers on the street nearly breaks double digits; their assailants not some anomalous sliver of their world, but rather saturating the field. Women are routinely attacked, carrying the constant *threat* of such attacks as a baseline bit of vigilance; a default feature of emotional life. Indefinitely. Without meaningful spatial limitations. Without meaningful refuge in which to even *exhale*.

And *nothing*. No crisis. No threat to public life perceived. No collective obligation to accommodate that terror *together*, or under-

take measures against it. It's not even *named*. The experiences of
those who shoulder the emotional and psychological labor of surviving that onslaught simply don't count. It is an extraordinary feat
of collective denial. And it makes moments like the Beltway sniper
saga seem childish and wildly lacking in perspective.

13

LUBE: IT'S NOT JUST FOR SEX ANYMORE

For just under ninety days, in the spring of 1998, I worked in D.C.'s now defunct LGBT bookstore. I was underemployed, and spotted their flyer offering slightly better-than-minimum-wage pay, plus benefits, while out with housemates at the District's long-mourned vegetarian haunt and sometimes punk venue, Food for Thought.

"Did they ask if you're straight?"

I knew this would be my mom's first question. Oddly, my prior employment at a bookstore in the Georgetown Park mall hadn't prompted questions about whether I was banging the bored wives of congressmen.

"No, why would they? Also, I'm not. It's a pretty stupid, meaningless category, no?"

Without realizing it, I was already feeling averse to more traditional—say, my mom's, or even those conventionally understood as "progressive"—notions of sexuality: building an identity around what sort of friction gets one off had come to seem pretty dubious.

The only reason such preferences mattered more than, say, what you soap up first in the shower, is that certain people convinced other people that what one does with one's genitals tells some disproportionately deep truth about who one is.

"Wait. What do you mean—you're not straight? What are you telling me?"

This is why the coming-out process almost never involves the phrase, "Mom . . . Dad . . . I like having my pucker consensually and capably fucked." We're relatively clear on the fact that such joys, in and of themselves, aren't really any of our business and have negligible impact on where our lives overlap. Unless our lives overlap in someone's asshole. But the conspicuously nebulous secret supposedly embedded in that confession? We harbor an inexplicable entitlement to and have proven ourselves abundantly amenable to routinely *destroying* people over it. Even though that secret is about as real as Santa Claus.

"Come on, mom. You can't possibly believe I made it to adulthood without ever having sexual contact with another male. You're not that naïve."

(*Long. Awkward. Pause.*)

"Well, whose pud were *you* pulling?"

I held the phone away, forcing hysterical laughter into as inaudible a sound as I could manage.

"Do you really want the answer to that question?"

"No."

"Probably for the best. Good talk, mom."

This was still a whole half-decade before the abolition of sodomy laws in the United States, and the internet was not yet user driven in ways that easily facilitated the formation of virtual communities. The District still technically had laws against "fornication" on the books. So spaces like bookstores were deeply necessary. A refuge. We were forbidden from censoring anything, or hanging up on anyone who called, as a boundary against perpetuating the shaming people faced on the outside. It turned out a friend of mine was dating the assistant manager, and she'd call in anytime I was working, sending me searching the magazine section for specifically dated copies of *Latin Inches*, and then subjecting me to incredibly graphic lines of questioning as to how my anatomy compared. To which I was required by store policy to respond with a not at all conspicuous, "I'm sorry, I can't give you that information," while coworkers and customers alike looked on.

The only employee manual I was ever given pertained to lube. The various brands and varieties we stocked, their qualities, the uses for which they were best suited, etc. Water-based (condom-compatible) vs. oil-based. Goopy vs. runny. "JO" (for solo use) vs. the stuff with the Ben Gay–esque warming agent, that you scoop out like pomade (the label read "elbow grease"). I had to memorize all of it. The shop didn't sell sex toys or the other sorts of things you'd find in a sex shop, but it sold lube. A *lot* of lube. Like, gallons. Daily. I know this because I was literally handing off half-gallon bottles, affixed with hand pumps. And not only to gay men. To lesbians. The odd hetero couple, even. I quickly deduced that anal sex

was a grossly underreported activity, and I became somewhat hyperaware of it happening *all around me*. You know when someone
points out something in a picture, and thereafter you can't *not* see
it? Like that. Except what I couldn't not see was people balls- and/or
elbow-deep in each other's backsides.

This meant that throughout any given day at my job, I was navigating transactions with customers that involved an intimacy most
of my friendships did not. Counseling complete strangers on how to
optimize, prolong, and better tailor to their desires a pleasure taboo
bound up with everything from social condemnation and religious
guilt, to deviance, emasculation, and . . . well . . . *excrement*. And
yet, in a twist perhaps worthy of a sociology dissertation, I learned
quickly that there was a bright boundary for most people around
actually acknowledging the act itself in any explicit way. Something
about it was too tender, too vulnerable to be named. It was as if to go
to the source, the very fulcrum upon which these detailed and often
clinically graphic conversations turned, was to excavate and color
saturate every desperate, normalizing act of physical and emotional
violence suffered by the person to whom I was speaking. Understandably, some tiny kernel of their experience needed to remain
unambiguously and safely *theirs*. It was never a tension we openly
discussed, but it was always present, always palpable.

The delicate verbal dance this required was not unlike pushing
two magnets together. I nonetheless learned it; how to anticipate
and assuage anxieties someone could not be brought to verbalize;
how to take seriously and tend to desires that could be owned in

one moment, effaced in another; how to affirm and usher someone's attention toward the unequivocal dignity of joy, while pirouetting through a minefield of self-hatred and stigma. A sodomy Sherpa, if you will.

I was eventually given a week to quit, or else be fired. It turns out that, whatever "liberatory" claims an enterprise can make for itself, some things *are* shameful. Namely, the comedian Leah De-laria's stand-up routine about Reagan's AIDS legacy and her reference to spite-fisting the former First Lady and impersonating her as a sock puppet. This apparently wasn't in-store stereo appropriate, notwithstanding the fact that we *sold* it. The management was also shorting the pay of the one Latina they had on staff, presumably thinking she wouldn't speak up and that the rest of us wouldn't care. The day of Youth Pride, on which the store was annually beset upon by jubilant throngs of queer teens, I bought four books on my employee discount and promptly walked off the job.

What I held on to, though, was that ability to discern when it was advantageous to perform an understanding of something that would otherwise compromise someone's modesty. I discovered very quickly, especially as I later phased out of working for pet-care agencies and into building my own freelance client base, that competency as a dog walker can be measured almost entirely by that very intuition. Run a cursory search for pet-care businesses in a given U.S. city, and you're *bound* to come across an ungodly number of names you wouldn't be caught dead saying out loud. *Waggy Walkies*, or some similarly cringe-worthy atrocity on the English language. If you're in the market for someone with whom to entrust your animal companion's well-being for some portion of each day, the first thing you're going to do is wonder whether whoever came up with that name was recently struck in the face with a heavy object. The second thing you're going to do is *wish* such a fate upon them, just before you resume looking for a dog walker.

This inability to glean that a client is in the market for a service with which they will heretofore be *associated*—if only in their own minds—has ramifications beyond your having failed to notice you're marketing the care of a living thing and not the services of a birthday clown or some new diaper wipe. It suggests you're oblivious; that you won't notice things of real import, in situations with potentially fatal consequences. But more subtly, it betrays an oblivious lack of regard for the client. At minimum, their encounter with you should not compromise their self-respect.

And it's here that that attention really counts: human-animal relationships are incredibly weighted, emotionally complex things. The fact that a client has reached out to you at all suggests they care about this weird, furry thing in ways that involve some degree of projection. They see themselves reflected in their animal. They very likely perceive and deeply *believe in* far more personality in their dog than is cognitively plausible. They baby-talk to it. They make sacrifices for it that are well out of proportion with a being that will be lucky to live more than a decade in many cases. And when that relationship comes to a close, they will be reduced to an absolute mess—probably within earshot and line of sight of professional colleagues, dating prospects, and children too young to see them as anything but invincible. The reasons for them to fear the real risk of embarrassment in how they relate to this little being are manifold. And at the end of the day, this emotional intensity is precisely what allows dog walkers to command the price point that they do. It should be *honored*. Not in some cynical preservation of a dog walker's economic self-interest, but because humans digging deep and risking that for the joy that *is* empathy is a fucking gift. It is what holds back the monsters at the gate: the flicker of an immune response to the worst of what humans have brought into this world. It is not to be trifled with.

If you're not willing to accept and honor that that is, in even its silliest manifestations, absolutely *sacred*, you have no business in the trade, and you should promptly—for everyone's benefit— get the fuck out. More still, you should humor whatever modesty is required for someone to wade into that adventure. That means learning how to *perform* client consultations. Deftly. Attentively. Disarmingly.

14

INDICATOR SPECIES

As the demand for dog walking has grown in particularly dense, gentrifying urban centers, many an entrepreneur has seized upon it as a scalable service enterprise like any other. It isn't, and when the MBAs get going, an often illustrative bit of unwitting self-parody results, on a variety of fronts.

First, there is an open presumption of expendability when it comes to workers. Large-scale pet daycare and dog-walking agencies in New York City advertise weekly open interviews with candidates for whom they've seen not so much as a resume, signaling to workers their own precarity, and to clients an evidently epic turnover rate. The former is an extreme version of a longstanding and common tactic in retail industries. Management continues to advertise openings or accept applications even when fully staffed, so as to discipline their workers through a constant, enforced vulnerability. The latter reflects an utter lack of self-awareness and an obliviousness about the service they're offering or how to market it. Setting aside the risks this sloppy vetting poses—both for the safety of living things, and the security of clients' homes—dogs are incredibly sensitive beings, with often complex needs and interests. Stability in their relationships is of a premium. The only reason a service provider wouldn't advertise their sensitivity to these considerations is that they *don't get them*. At all.

At the same time, the lack of barriers to entry in the trade tends to attract some very questionable members of the managerial class. No qualifications are required; one needn't even have ever so much as *looked* at a dog. Often, these businesses are acquired through purchase. So cluelessness and self-infatuation make for a dangerous combination: grown adults acting the part they bought their way into, as though sticking a card in your bike spokes makes you Evel Knievel. I've had agency interviews where owners courted me with the delusional "genius" of their expansion into online pet-supply retail or nebulous pet-care certification credentialing services, with negligibly little explanation or sense of why any of what they were selling was even desirable (much less competitive with existing models). Another feigned to contract me as a consultant, when she discovered her underpaid, overworked staff was cutting corners (mostly, skipping walks), a situation paired with abysmal employee retention, which put her at risk of being unable to meet the needs of her existing clients. I asked if she'd considered paying them more, or perhaps offering benefits or some profit-sharing structure. She countered with the suggestion I cover her existing labor gap, at the same shitty pay the rest of her staff apparently resented. Perhaps most telling of all, I was once asked to interview my potential employer, as though their fascinating responses would be sufficient compensation for my time, prior to even being hired.

A recurrent and rarely understood feature of commercial dog-walking outfits is the noncompete clause as a standard, baseline condition of employment. In effect, in exchange for any hope of being hired, an applicant is compelled to sign a document that enables their would-be employer to sue them for continuing to work as a dog walker after ceasing to work for the company in question. This cuts against the most classic models of work-experience acquisition, effectively giving a single employer outright *ownership* of their workforce's relevant skillset. It also applies a de facto downward pressure on wages: one cannot translate one's skills into a better opportunity, and one's knowledge and ability of a given trade effectively dissolve into thin air when not generating revenue for a *specific* employer.

Worse still, structuring a business this way hobbles quality control, by immunizing an already undemocratic scenario. A smaller agency I worked for had two tiers: the owner, and the four of us working for her. The back-end, administrative dimension of the outfit was totally opaque; we showed up and worked the schedule of dogs we were given each day. Twice in as many weeks, my boss failed to put a certain client on my schedule. The first time, she offered to pay for the rug the dog pissed on while locked in the house all day. The second, the client was prepared to move to another service. All of this was out of view for those of us doing the actual work. So I was surprised when I ran into this particular client one day and she mentioned the firing of a coworker I was absolutely certain did not exist. Rather than be transparent with our clients, and own mistakes or lapses in service, our boss had *invented* a worker, blamed him for the problem, and positioned herself as the responsible proprietor by assuring the client that this slacker had been canned. Given that I had performed reliably and to the satisfaction of the client, I clearly stood to offer a better service, working with her directly. This would've been mutually beneficial in that I'd have been entitled to the full value of the invoice, as opposed to working for a wage. I was not bound by a noncompete (our boss was hardly so attentive to detail), but had I been, such a solution would've been cause for a disorganized, dishonest business owner to sue one or even the both of us. Regardless, even revealing I knew this story to be 100 percent bullshit would've cost me my job.

Noncompetes also ensure, in perpetuity, an unskilled labor pool. If one cannot take one's skills elsewhere, only those with *no* skills will apply to work. And on the flip side, businesses will only *hire* those with no experience, for fear of being sued under a noncompete. Conventional logic would dictate this is a terrible marketing strategy, but employers are increasingly confident their customers are too stupid and undiscerning to ferret this out. Indeed, according to *The New York Times*, noncompete clauses are steadily proliferating to unlikely trades. Editors, landscapers, yoga teachers, personal trainers, hair stylists—even *interns* are being slapped with and bound to bans on working in the field for which they're apprenticing. Which means that you can be enticed to provide free labor for a period of time, in anticipation of and as an investment toward future employment, and if an employer simply decides they'd rather just *not* pay a *new* someone for the same period of time, stringing together desperate, unpaid workers indefinitely, they can even bar you from being paid for that same labor elsewhere. Typically, these clauses have expiration dates or geographic limits. But it ultimately doesn't matter. With innovation in so many fields moving at such rapid pace, returning to work from which you've been barred for six months to two years means you might as well move on.

It's also not uncommon for a dog-walking agency to be but one limb in a small empire. The second agency I worked for launched a housecleaning service, doubling the value of its existing client base, while replicating the lucrative cost-minimal structure of a staff comprised entirely of contractors. The lack of real overhead in both trades likely resulted in capital sufficient to finance other such ventures. And on and on. Much as Amazon's business model is built around monetizing consumer data—and an almost contemptuous indifference to the products it sells—the landscape of commercial dog walking is more often than not breathtakingly cynical, despite literally selling care for living beings. The correspondence between these two disparate iterations of enterprise suggests a lack of novelty to any of it. It is, in effect, the world we wake up to; the air we breathe; the orientation of those with decision-making power expressed with greater or lesser degrees of candor. Dog walking being so unencumbered by any real standards or accountability, its entrepreneur class can avail themselves of a sometimes stunning lack of subtlety.

So, as an exercise in meeting entrepreneurial logic on its own terms, and foregrounding its brazen contempt for the intelligence of others and the actual content of the human activities it colonizes, below I've answered the job application questions featured on the website of one of New York City's largest dog-walking agencies.

You're welcome.

Do you have an iPhone or smartphone? [Y/N]

I have an iPhone. My friend unlocked it for me after I couldn't pay the bill anymore. So now I have prepay service through another carrier (and a new number the bill collectors from the last one don't know about). I rarely get better than an edge signal in New York City, and occasionally let the service lapse in favor of eating. Hope that's okay.

iMessage still works when I've got wifi. So if *you've* got an iPhone, we're all good.

Sex: [Male/Female]

I have a penis, but I'm guessing any dog would figure that out pretty quickly. Good lookin' out.

What is your background with animals? (Did you have pets growing up, if so what kinds and breeds, have you ever given medication to an animal if yes what kind, do you have pets currently, have you ever volunteered at animal shelter, petsat for friends/family if yes list details of breeds)

I've been a dog walker for over a decade. So I can confidently say both that I've given most varieties of medication to dogs/cats, and that the details of the breeds I grew up around factor precisely zero in any background you should be interested in, if you've ever done this job or live on planet Earth. Asking about breeds makes you look like a pretentious ass-hat, totally winging it at a care trade. It's a lousy strategy. Here are a few questions of *actual* relevance you might've asked, instead:

- Do have full use of your limbs?
- Can you handle walking nonstop for four to six hours, in all local weather conditions?
- How many times have you lost your keys? Be honest.
- Can you manage a finicky lock without completely losing your shit?
- Have you ever been told you have anger-management issues?
- True or false? Bodily functions are absolutely hilarious.
- Did you grow up in a community where dogs were weaponized by police or other security outfits, to terrify or coerce people?
- Have you been otherwise traumatized by experiences with dogs?
- Can you explain the difference between a choke collar and a pinch collar? Do you know which is more humane?

*Are you currently working (please list any things you do that pay
$$ even if its [sic] not full time, and how much per week you make
doing it) if yes what are you doing and what days/hours do you do
it, this is a supplementary income so we need to be confident you
can do this for at least 6 months as this won't pay your rent.*

It's relatively uncontroversial that a central cost of doing business
is the reproduction of one's workforce. (Even Adam Smith thought
so.) By that, I mean compensating workers at such a nominal rate
that you don't find yourself short a guy on account of his having
shuffled off from starvation or exposure after last clocking out.
Shelter seems a pretty nonnegotiable provision, here.

If I understand the question correctly, explicit conditions of my
employment with your operation are as follows:

- I acknowledge you will *not* pay me enough to cover my
  rent.
- I supply you with *detailed* confirmation of some outside
  subsidy to your extracting surplus value from my labor.

What you're actually saying here is that neoliberalism has ap-
parently gone so off the rails that the role of "job creator" has been
stripped of its usefulness to society. A job, according to this rubric,
is something contingent on *another* job (or even a third job!), or
(more likely) externally held debt. That, or you're an astoundingly
brazen piece of shit that any workforce would rightfully lock in a
closet, for eternity.

It's telling that the assumption at work in all of this is "such are

the conditions of the market; if you can't hang, don't work here."
There's a sort of moral weight applied in this calculation, shoul-
dered entirely by workers. (Every time you hear a pundit speak with
smarmy confidence about "worker flexibility," you're encountering
the same thing.) We're supposed to feel stupid and naïve for thinking we deserve to survive, and recalibrate our sense of worth ac-
cordingly.

But it's unclear to me why the logic doesn't tilt in another direction. Perhaps: "Them's the breaks. If you can't do business without
a subsidy, GTFO." Or, "Here's the deal: If your business requires
collective risk, the price of admission is collective administration
and reward-distribution." *But what the fuck do I know?* I'm just a
dog walker.

For the sake of argument, I'll stick to what's appropriate to my
calling. The vast majority of demand in this trade falls between the
hours of 11 a.m. and 4 p.m.—the middle chunk of the average work-
a-day job. You know, the kind your clients have, preventing them
from being home to walk their own dogs. That'll likely break down
thus:

11:00–11:30
Four dogs grouped from separate households, billed at $19 each.
TOTAL: $76

11:30–12:00
Four dogs, two from one household at a 25 percent discount.
TOTAL: $66.50

Then multiplied by five, for an average daily gross of $712.50, and a per-minute rate of about $2.38. From *one worker*, among an *armada*. None of whose rent you can cover. The U.S. Bureau of Labor Statistics puts the average hourly wage of a dog walker at $9.60, which you'll pay under a 1099, absolving you of any costs associated with workers' income taxes, even though you treat them as employees in every other way. This could as much as *halve* their take-home pay.

And since they'll be showing up during the bulk of the standard business day, whatever second or third gig they'll be working to afford the privilege of making one tenth of what they're generating for you will have to fit into the hours that remain. So your clients can expect them to be overworked, underslept, maybe drug addled (to power through all these work hours, or to cope with the stress of managing it all), inattentive, and *broke*—thus prone to cutting corners on the job, neglecting dogs, forgetting to lock doors, or even stealing from clients' homes. They can also expect rampant turnover, meaning the stability that companion animals typically require is out the window, and about the only quality control you can offer is some Orwellian GPS tracking app you're installing on your workers' smartphones (which, by the way, constitute a subsidy to your business model, as you're not paying for the devices). They should probably expect their walker to endure the odd stress fracture, or other repetitive stress injury, as well.

Why should clients *expect* all that, you ask? Oh I don't know.

Maybe because you're announcing it on your site, with this down-right *insane* application form.

Do you have any planned trips out of town in next 3–4 months (if yes please list exact dates, any weddings, vacations, business trip, visiting friends or family)?
To be honest, with all the rent I won't be able to pay, I was kinda just gonna pass my nights on the subway. So no travel beyond the more scenic corners of the five boroughs.

What specific neighborhood do you currently live in, will you be moving in the next 6 months, are you on a lease if yes when does it expire?
C'mon. This is just . . . Well, actually, you're aware that *punctuation* is a thing, right?

Look, the subtext of this question is pretty clear. If your business's viability is so reliant upon the stability of my living arrangement, that is *literally* a textbook cost of doing business, for you. If you're not in a position to cover that financially, you're not looking for an employee; you're looking for an investor—investment in the form of uncompensated labor. Sweat equity. Only, you're not offering me any stake in the return. If my investment of labor in your enterprise performs well, I will see nothing. And your reliance on my investment will afford me no decision-making power or input. It's insulting to everyone's intelligence that you think it appropriate to subtly admonish my precarity in the

same breath with which you openly declare your intent to perpetu-
ate it.

What are your hobbies? What are your dreams and aspirations?
Where do you see yourself in a year?

Dog walkers are broadly intelligible as creatives covering material
bases in a manual trade while carrying out various unpaid labors of
love in their downtime. Music, art, theater, writing, comedy. As stereotypes go, this one actually has some basis in truth. And it's precisely why so many dog-walking agencies feature profiles of their
employees waxing exuberant about how when Jonathan isn't stroll-
ing pups around Park Slope, he's a music producer in Bushwick. Or
how, prior to pet care, Ashley did an MFA and has choreographed
performances at P.S. 122 in recent years.

The dreams and aspirations of your workforce are free marketing content for your website. And you know it. Abstractions of their
creative work—ignoring its content entirely—are sold to your clients, alongside the manual labor that won't even finance their most
basic necessities. And yet, you're terrified of the incredibly unlikely
prospect that one of them might catch a break and be able to con-
vert their *actual* creative output into compensation for which you
cannot play parasite. The audacity coursing through all that stuns
the senses, really.

Which brings me to a final point: inasmuch as you have stopped
just shy of declaring you give not a single fuck whether I live or
die, *my dreams and aspirations are none of your fucking business.*
You're not entitled to that sort of intimacy with me, no matter how

badly you want to paper over the crudely extractive relation you're attempting to establish, here. Your "care" means shit to me, and does not stand in for my survival.

To quote a celebrated Scorsese film immortalizing the sentiments of the very criminal manifestations of capitalism your racket embodies: *Fuck you. Pay me.*

15

EVEN STATE DEPARTMENT STAFFERS GET THE BLUES

"Heyyyyyyyy. You're here!"

The exuberance felt out of place to me, but then again, people who hire dog walkers are a fairly broad sample set. You encounter all types, and when you *do* actually meet clients face to face, the context clues by which you might navigate other exchanges tend to flee the scene. While *you* are technically on the job, and thus bound by some intelligible set of behavioral parameters, clients are not. Often times, they're just caught between the formalities of a professional encounter and the casual behaviors to which they're inclined in their own homes—and the latter often comes more naturally. The familiarity of their own environment yields a predictable entitlement to that at-ease inertia—and a given client's at-ease could be *anything*. The initial consultation is always an away game. There are no reliable common denominators. The odds you'd even know the person you're pitching suffered a *stroke* five minutes before you arrived are relatively slim.

I rarely had occasion to meet coworkers' clients. Pretty much the only circumstance under which such introductions were made was when someone was out of pocket for one reason or another, and an unusually jumpy client wanted to meet the walker subbing in. This particular evening was such an occasion. A duplex. A woman employed with the State Department in some fashion. I'd been to the house before, even met the dog; a young, practically inexhaustible Boston, obsessed with fetching. But the client he lived with was a total stranger to me. And it might've been better for everyone involved had she remained so.

"God, I'm really sorry. Do you guys think my house is okay? Should I arrange the furniture differently?"

I once briefly walked a puppy for a couple on Capitol Hill, both with careers in warmongering. Him, a marine. Her, some position or another at the Pentagon. I remember being perched atop the toilet in the half-bathroom off their living room, reading the back-cover synopsis of some ridiculous, almost certainly vanity-published work they had on hand about how the Muslim world hates the West because it feels emasculated by the latter's surpassing the once great Islamic contributions to math, science, and (probably) soap. I don't, however, have the foggiest recollection of what the place looked like. I was *far* more likely to giddily text friends evidence of a client's terrible taste in literature than I was their interior decor, if only because the former better served the ends of skewering meritocracy. "Six fucking figures. And she reads at a *Harry Potter* level!" And even still, none of that had any bearing whatsoever on whether or not I'd hang with their dog or take their money. I'd walked dogs for trust-fund Georgetown grads and DoD employees—people with sufficient means to have their shit together, or at least a well-guarded vanity—whose homes resembled the aftermath of a tactical SWAT detonation. There's only so long you can indulge astonishment at such things without being forced to choose between emotional exhaustion, or a revised understanding of median adulthood.

I knew her question wasn't really *about* that, though. Especially as my years in the trade wore on, client consultations meant being face to face with people more or less my age. And they were often visibly ambivalent about their lives, prone to projecting some mixture of "cool"—and whatever of that they imagined they'd forfeited—onto mine. There was a lot of needless apologizing and contrived shame over nominal affluence performed in my presence, as though my approval conferred some exemption from the character of their compromises; as though my opinion of anyone's lifestyle mattered in any equation whatsoever; or as though I wasn't fully aware of why they'd pursued particular comforts and even shared in their appreciation of them. Upon learning I was her age and in the process of getting divorced, one client—a married woman staffing for a prominent Democratic senator—inexplicably turned wistful and blurted out "I feel like I've done nothing with my life!" Such exchanges became so routine that I half-wondered how many of my clients were writing me checks each week for access to some vicarious sense of what amounted, for them, to adventure or conversation pieces at Hill happy hours. "Our dog walker went to *Palestine*! Yeah, crazy, right?"

The Boston, beside himself at my coworker's off-time visit and unable to contain his elation, was by all appearances halfway to a full-on seizure. "Does he behave okay? Should I be doing something differently in training him?" On the surface, not an altogether odd inquiry, coming from a client. They frequently mistook us for dog *trainers*, likely unaware that such credentials would command a considerably higher price point. But this particular evening, in practically the same breath as her soliciting our input on her furniture arrangement, the question felt more loaded; like she was just nervously fumbling through prompts, unaware that their cumulative effect was an embarrassing, barely veiled scramble for the approval of two tattooed young men, sweaty from biking across town. It suddenly hit me that her eyes were reddish and puffy. I tried to change the subject, asking about the dog's typical daily routine.

"Well, we usually take him to the park around the corner first thing, on weekends . . . I mean . . . Ugh, I guess I have to stop saying 'we' now."

I shot a stern, wide-eyed sideways glance at my coworker, half-suspicious that he *knew* we were walking into the wake of a breakup and thought it'd be funny not to tell me. Worse, my attempt to diffuse an awkward situation and steer us back into practical terrain had uncorked an excruciating tailspin from which we would never recover.

"Oh, I should show you the guest room, so you know where you'll be staying."

I leapt at her suggestion, if only because leaving my coworker in the living room meant one less set of eyes on her and her steadily more embarrassing meltdown. When she turned to me at the top of the steps, I could smell the booze. I fought every muscle in my face, suppressing a visible shudder.

I let her show me the room, and nodded while hearing absolutely nothing she said, as she went over what I'm sure were self-evident details. "So," she said, having burned through all relevant topics of discussion, stepping awkwardly into my personal space, "Blake tells me you write? What do you write about?" *Fuck.* The last place I needed to be was standing at the foot of a bed, casually queried about what I did with my downtime by a drunkenly oblivious thirty-something on the rebound, who gave every indication of having completely lost the plot. I hadn't actually written anything beyond a few pieces for anarchist journals, and discussing them with a State Department employee was almost certainly among the least interesting ways I could imagine spending even a few fleeting seconds of my evening. My coworker had probably just checked off whatever conventional details he could convey over the phone when scheduling our introduction, to make me seem interesting and un-threatening. In his wildest dreams nothing he'd relayed would ever have become fodder for the world's most untimely and inappropriate attempt at rebound-seduction. Under no circumstances would I egg her on, humoring the discussion. I noticed the dog had followed us upstairs, and was out of frame from where she stood, so I pretended he was up to something that required intervention, as an excuse to derail her. "Maybe we should get you back downstairs before you get into something you shouldn't."

There was relief in saying it out loud, even if directed at the dog.

Rounding the base of the stairs, back into the living room, I locked eyes with my coworker, futilely trying to convey the code red in which we were immersed, but before I could steer the encounter to a speedy close, our host lobbed a verbal drunk-grenade into the whole thing.

"You guys are really smart, you know? Have you ever thought about taking the Foreign Service exam?"

We silently stared at her, hostage to the realization that she was twice as likely to pass out and come crashing through the coffee table at our feet as she was to realize the lunacy of what she'd just said. Neither seemed in the offing. My coworker laughed, nervously, then went for broke.

"Uh, no. That's about the worst idea ever."

She was undeterred, firmly convinced of her own genius, in that way only inebriation allows.

"No. Listen for a sec . . . The State Department represents all Americans. All of 'em! We want diversity."

She was slurring, now. Vaguely combative. And she'd mysteriously concluded that two hetero-passing white guys would really shake up the State Department's workplace demographics. I wouldn't have minded the few hundred bucks she was worth to me, but the whole encounter had gone so sideways that nothing mattered in that moment beyond getting the fuck *out* of her house and preempting some full-blown catastrophe. We were already well off the rails.

"Look. I have an FBI file," I said. "Not maybe. Definitely. I know because my fingerprints were put straight into the FBI database; it's standard when you're arrested on federal charges. I'm pretty sure that rules me out."

She went somber, pensive—in that Kathy-Bates-in-*Misery* sort of way.

"What'd you do?"

I was suddenly *very* aware that I was talking to an agent of the State, and may have just kicked a hornets' nest of surveillance and official harassment. But I was set on forking the whole shit-show, and was ready to bet on her pulling very little weight in whatever professional role she held.

"I shut down an embassy. And my passport's flagged with a major U.S. ally."

She stared off at nothing, as though I'd just told her I was her son.

"This could have ramifications for me, for my job."

In reality, it couldn't. My mom retired near the top of the civil-service pay scale, a career DoD employee. By the spring of 2001, when her security clearance was up for review and the FBI dispatched an agent to interview me over tea in Dupont Circle, I'd been arrested more than a handful of times, more than once on federal property of some sort (including one major military base). In late 1997, some agency or another had seen fit to plaster every university in northwest D.C. with flyers encouraging people interested in "killing cops and making incendiary devices" to attend a conference on civil disobedience that I was helping organize. Conveniently, the only number that appeared on these flyers was mine; a fact that wasn't lost on the intelligence division of the D.C. police, who interviewed me for a solid two hours. The spring of 2000, the FBI had stationed an agent in the group house upstairs from the apartment I shared with two other local anarchists; all of us hip deep in plans to shut down the spring meetings of the International Monetary Fund and World Bank. For one piece of our organizing, my housemate had cobbled together a list of the limo companies contracted to shuttle delegates to the meetings, and had begun planning to dispatch groups to lock down on each company's lot for the first morning. Before we could set any of it in motion, our apartment was broken into, with no signs of forced entry, and the only thing missing was said list. An enraged phone call followed from our landlord, who turned out to be some sort of Turkish closet fascist—a higher-up with the Ataturk Society of America. "I know what you're doing!" he shouted. Clearly, whatever agency had stolen our scouting notes had collaborated with him to gain access to our home. Hence the lack of forced entry.

But Mom's security clearance was still somehow kosher. My hanging out with a dog and sleeping in the home of a State Department staffer, by comparison, was unlikely to raise even the quietest alarms. But this woman didn't need to know that. I offered half-hearted assurances, and my coworker and I took the lull in her meltdown as a window through which to exit, almost without a word.

Her voicemail beat us to our destination. A jumbled, stammering mess of sentence fragments, the thrust of which was that she didn't need a dog sitter, after all.

Thank fuck.

16

IN WHICH WE ALL LEARN A VALUABLE LESSON ABOUT SCHEDULING

Clients routinely schedule walks they wind up not needing, and they're then surprised to see some person keying into their front door. No one expects a stranger to just key into their front door, unannounced. It's the stuff of psycho-thrillers. And it's usually about the only reason you see your clients in person, after an initial consultation. A certain unweighted intimacy usually results—the kind of thing you don't get to inhabit with many people on a daily basis. Safely holding that experience, between near strangers, can be profoundly humanizing. It's the stuff we're told can't happen; the reason we have home security systems, don't talk to strangers, and think it anything but patently absurd when cops shoot unarmed people.

Given what he got up to, it was probably more a personal day than a sick day.

The apartment's layout was atypical; the bulk of it recessed be-

low the main entrance, with a set of stairs between, so that the first
few feet inside figured as a sort of balcony overlooking the living
room. Directly below, out of view to the entrance, was the sitting
area. A couch, a recliner, some side tables. Standard stuff. The far
wall, all mirrors. Who knew what for? Maybe a dancer had bought
and renovated the place at some point. Whatever its function, it
clearly mattered little to him. He'd assembled an entertainment
center against it, outfitted with a sizable flat-screen TV, leaving only
limited glimpses of the room reflected in the mirrors' margins at
the edges of the wall.

He made coffee. Listened to NPR's *Morning Edition* while feeding the dogs. Then walked them to the nicer of the neighborhood's
dog parks, near the top of Seventeenth Street NW, just below U
Street. It was fenced in, Astroturfed, and laid out as a sort of knoll,
so that a daily hosing would rinse all accumulated residue downhill
into the surrounding mulch. He mingled, threw a ball, played with
a few dogs he recognized. And then he cycled out of the rotation of
visitors, per routine.

He was one of the legacy members of the area's gay history, and
as that community began to disperse or migrate eastward, the dog
park served to highlight the neighborhood's changing demographics. There wasn't much tension per se, but the dog park increasingly
became one of the few noncommercial spaces in which public life
unfolded—a fact that was true of most dog parks, actually. One
learned as much about what was happening in the neighborhood
from conversations there as one did at community forums staged

by city council members, and one could estimate property values and local rates of telecommuting by simply observing the waves of people gathering there throughout the day.

After dropping the dogs off at home, he hit the gym, grabbing iced coffee on the walk home. It was 10:30 a.m. He still hadn't remembered to call the dog walker to cancel for the day. Under the best of conditions, this was an annoyance to the walker. It's fairly standard for clients, when first hiring a walker, to stipulate a time they'd like their dog walked. And any walker who tells a client they'll show up at an appointed time is a liar. Dogs themselves are unpredictable. Weather affects how one routes one's day. Urban life conspires against you at every turn.

And then there are the dogs you don't *need* to walk, but don't *know* you don't need to walk them, because a client neglected to tell you. So you budget your time and movements to accommodate what amounts to a null value. Depending on the client, you may have walked three dogs a half mile through the rain to reach a house you didn't need to be at. You may have already been a half hour behind schedule, because some dog was crated with explosive diarrhea that morning, and while you're not the client's housemaid, *not* cleaning up the disaster that greeted you before recrating the poor pup would be grounds for criminal prosecution. Cancellations are the crumpled twenty you find while doing laundry. They can be the difference between a decent day, and ripping your hair out.

She was probably circling her group from Seventeenth, maybe R Street, hooking them on a loop across Connecticut Avenue, down

Twentieth and back eastward via Q Street. Checking her phone for the time, mentally routing her day, plotting a coffee stop on Fourteenth at some point. He was toweling off from his shower, with the bathroom door wide open. The dogs chewing on toys in the hallway, expectant. They were probably surprised when he didn't beat his normal path to the bedroom's walk-in closet; not dressing as he normally did following such rituals. Curious, they followed him to the living room. The cast iron encircling his building, much as with most such District residences, doubled as dog parking. Unlike other cities, D.C. thankfully wasn't such a hot spot for dog theft, probably on account of it being so small. Short of fleeing the city with one's captive, it'd be hard to conceal such an act. Community LISTSERVs and blogs functioned with a sometimes staggering efficiency, for better or worse. Regardless, leashing dogs outside an apartment building was common practice, and most passersby would be wary of going near them. She threaded the leashes through a few of the bars and hooked the hand loops over the top of one post, shortening the lengths enough to prevent any real trouble from the dogs. She had no need of the front-door key, drifting in behind a UPS worker on delivery, both of them brushing past the mailman.

He'd brought the towel with him, figuring he might as well. He was still a bit damp, and it was better than getting the couch wet. The flat-screen booted up across the room. He fished the lube from a drawer in the side table, and began scrolling through pay-per-view. Some leather-daddy fare. She wound her way through the faux-industrial decor of the common areas and hallways, toward the apartment. An elevator bell dinged a few yards back. As her key hit the door, he instinctively scrambled for his phone, but quickly realized there was nothing to be done and nowhere to go. Her first gaze into the apartment met his eyes in the foot-wide sliver of mirror on the far wall. His shoulders rounded, he was leaning slightly forward. Midstroke, death grip. The dogs' heads spun upward toward the landing. An "Oh my god" spilled out of her, with as much volume as can be managed in a gasp. The door slammed shut.

He found his phone, feverishly thumbing through its address book for the agency's number. Thankfully, it was owned by a friend. He never got to say a word.

"Dave. I already know."

17

THE WYOMING

Near the corner of Nineteenth Street and Florida Avenue NW sits the Washington Hilton, where an attempt on former president Ronald Reagan's life was made in March of 1981, just over two months into his first term. While it remains a site of many high-profile events, political and otherwise, the hotel has never really escaped that day's shadow. To this day, one can find locals calling the hotel "The Hinckley Hilton," a reference to Reagan's shooter, John Hinckley Jr. Less an homage than a consequentialist moral evaluation; a *realpolitik*. However batshit Hinckley was, Reagan's impact on the world was so abominable and monstrous, even *inadvertent* tributes were untenable. While Reagan's breaking an air-traffic controller strike didn't prevent the federal government from naming Washington National Airport after him, it took nearly a decade, and a congressional threat of suspended funding, to force the D.C. Metro to include the name on station maps.

Set behind and overlooking the Hilton is the Wyoming, a sort of old-guard apartment structure at the eastern end of Columbia Road NW, the east–west corridor of Adams Morgan. In its layout, it's atypical of the District. Two freestanding ornate stone towers, straddling a ground-level lobby. It wouldn't be out of place on Manhattan's Upper East Side, the feel and culture of the building owing less to Adams Morgan, and more to the smattering of diplomatic outposts along the adjacent stretch of Connecticut Avenue running between Dupont Circle and Woodley Park. Just a few blocks to the north, one finds the Chinese Embassy; to the south and west, the near end of Massachusetts Avenue's "Embassy Row," which stretches all the way to the vice president's residence at the U.S. Naval Observatory.

My first clients in The Wyoming were a semiretired couple who easily could've been characters cast as the conscience of a Woody Allen film. Their apartment had a similar feel—an extensive, hardcover-heavy library in the sitting room; tasteful antique furniture—and was tellingly left unlocked, as a rule. They'd hired me when the husband, a former editor at a major newspaper, underwent knee surgery that made repeated walks throughout the day prohibitive. The wife had some role at one of the museums on the National Mall and wasn't always available to step in, so I was brought on as relief. Visits to their apartment bookended my days. I'd walk their dog to Eighteenth Street and grab coffee midmorning, then round out my day's route back at the Wyoming late afternoon, heading to the nearby gym afterward, or the public pool on the edge of Georgetown during the warmer months.

The afternoon walks often coincided with late-day routines in the building. Residents whose workdays ended on the earlier side, nannies carting toddlers back from the park up the street, or daily mail delivery. I wasn't allowed to hold keys, and had to be announced to my clients by the concierge, so the increased traffic at this hour often made for delays. During one such wait, I found myself standing next to Christopher Hitchens, the late public intellectual and author, perhaps most well known to my generation for his alcoholism and his practically birthing "New Atheism," a questionable tradition now upheld by noted assholes Richard Dawkins and Sam Harris. Prior to the 9/11 attacks, Hitchens had been something of a mainstay of left-wing intellectual life and human-rights discourse, authoring an impressive array of articles and other works, including a book written in collaboration with Palestinian literary critic Edward Said. Hitchens's polemicist tenacity and abrasive wit yielded a sort of scorched-earth orientation toward the hypocrisy and violence of Western imperialism. He didn't simply indict those he took to task. He *eviscerated* them, his bravado matched only by his lack of apology.

After 9/11, he became something else, entirely. Islamophobic, bloodthirsty, turning his rage on the very populations victimized by his former foes. Suddenly, the U.S. government whose backing was instrumental in the dictatorship of Pinochet for which he'd put Henry Kissinger on "trial" in one book was nobly inviolate in invading Afghanistan and Iraq. Ironically, after this turn he authored a work titled *Why Orwell Matters*.

I knew Hitchens to be a British national, and had no idea he lived in the United States, much less the District. I'd passed him on the street once, as he stumbled, red-faced and bleary-eyed, out of La Tomate, a bistro in Dupont Circle. My first thought was, Wow. That guy is really lit. Moments later, it hit me who he was. Since then, as a lifelong chain-smoker with few rivals, he'd been diagnosed with terminal throat cancer. His condition had been reported in the press, and he'd given a few interviews on it here and there, mostly to assure everyone that no road-to-Damascus conversion was in the offing. Standing in the lobby of The Wyoming, on the far side of chemotherapy, he was nearly unrecognizable. I began furtively texting my clients. "I'm downstairs. Am I standing next to fucking Christopher Hitchens?!" The reply came seconds later: "Oh yes. 'The Hitch' and his family have the largest unit in the building. We know them well."

The urge suddenly came over me to confront him. After all, I'd suffered beatings—as well as out-and-out torture—at the hands of cops while taking the streets for the causes by which he'd rose to prominence. I was ready to be escorted from the building, and subsequently fired. The words welled up in my throat, "Hey, guy. Help me out. I've always wondered: Where exactly do you keep your Orwell suit?" But looking at his pathetic, chemically battered form—one foot already in the grave—I realized it'd amount to little better than punching down (a pastime I was happy to forfeit to him). He was already gone. Already irrelevant. Withering away in an old apartment overlooking Dupont Circle, disowned by all but the proudly cynical. We made eye contact. I don't recall my exact expression, but *his* suggested that I'd given away my knowing contempt. He shuffled back to the elevator with his mail, while I waited to be announced by the concierge.

My second clients in The Wyoming were a couple living in its east tower, one a higher-up in a major labor union. I'd been referred to them by a friend working as one of the union's paralegals. They were more sporadic, given they were cat people, and only called on me when they were heading out of town and in need of check-ins for their rather skittish, elderly little lady. It was something of a fiasco, as the cat required thyroid medication that it avoided when placed in food. She hid from me every time I showed up, so administering meds proved a nonstarter. I remember going to great lengths to smash the pills on their counter with the butt of a butter knife and then distributing their powdered remnants in wet food so as to be minimally detectable. Usually, with little effect.

On one such visit, an early-evening stop I made en route to a friend's birthday dinner, I found a young woman of grad-school age waiting at the elevator. She was in running shorts and a nondescript T-shirt, as though she'd come from a run or the gym, and was eyeballing her mail. Her attire and age were conspicuous in that space. It was host to a mostly unspoken but nonetheless stifling decorum. I ventured she either inherited her place, or had some familial benefactor footing the bill. The Wyoming was *not* a grad-school residence, and no one so young would be far enough into their career to cover the cost of living there. The doors opened, and I followed her in.

"What floor?" she asked, reaching for the buttons.

"Uh, five. Thanks." I was always hyperaware of my outsider status in these spaces; the apprehension of residents who saw me as unfamiliar. On more than one occasion, unknown residents had complained about perfectly innocuous things I'd done, like somehow treading too loudly on the carpeted hallway of one floor at 10 a.m. I did my best to avoid taking up space or making anyone suspicious of my presence. In fact, I did my best to be pretty much invisible.

"That's *my* floor," she said, reaching to illuminate the corresponding button on the elevator's front wall.

"Great." I was rather inanely relieved not to cause her the additional labor of pressing another floor.

My first few years in the trade, I was treated to pretty much the same curiosity each time I disclosed what I did for a living. "You ever fuck any of your clients?" I never quite got my head around why this question occurred to anyone. "You do realize, don't you, that people typically hire me to do a thing they can't because they're *not home*, right?" Best I could deduce, dog walkers figured for many people much as pool boys have in literary and cinematic tropes. The key distinction between the two, much to the disappointment of anyone convinced of this unwieldy conflation, is that the work pool boys perform occurs *at* the home. My primary obligation was to get the fuck out of it. Ideally with one or more dogs in tow.

I certainly made friends with clients. Enduring friendships, even. In one case, while doing a morning walk for a small dog home alone for a night, I ran into the woman he lived with, home earlier than expected. She was a doctor in the trauma center at George Washington University Hospital who, given her digs, must've been transplanted into town on pretty quick notice. I'd had a number of clients in her building, which seemed to serve as sort of corporate short-term housing when law firms or the like needed to bring in someone for a month or so. The units often looked more like hotel suites than apartments. She was landing more permanently, but had been placed in one of them as an interim measure, I guessed. Presumably lacking much time for cultivating a social life in her new surroundings (given her job description), she queried me about why I liked the District. My day was open, so I offered to show her around. We wound up spending the day together. I couldn't tell if it was a date. She very well may have approached it as such. I didn't really care, and hadn't made the offer with that in mind. We kept our hands to ourselves, and I walked away with a free scrip for multiple refills on my asthma inhaler. This was, in effect, as close to anything sexual or romantic that I ever got up to with clients.

"You going to my place?" the grad student asked coyly, from the far side of The Wyoming's suddenly *very* cozy elevator. I felt guilty she was forced into such close quarters with me. I checked the clock on my phone. Nervously. There was no real risk I was late to my friend's birthday thing, but pretty much *any* distraction would've sufficed at that point, short of being able to disappear entirely. I was fairly certain she was just making light of my outsider status, inquiring as to whether I was up to something nefarious. Like stalking. It probably embarrassed her how eager I was to assuage what I'd read as concern, feigned as it may have been.

"Ah, no. I'm just going to feed someone's cat." Definitely stammered. Summoning all the stupid earnestness I'd somehow evaded during puberty.

We passed from three to four in silence. Clearly attuned to the timing of the elevator from floor to floor, she looked up just before the doors opened on five. Eyes trained on me. Like prey. All confidence and seriousness. "That's not nearly as exciting."

She turned back to her mail and coolly strolled out of the elevator.

It didn't even seem real. A sort of "Dear *Penthouse Forum* . . ." moment. As the evening wore on, I kept replaying the exchange in my head. Did that just happen? Do people do that? Certainly it was completely at odds with every other encounter I'd had in The Wyoming.

Christ, I thought to myself, actually laughing a little, as I rounded Columbia's downward slope onto Connecticut toward the Hilton. What would she have done if I'd said, "Actually, yes. I *am* going to your place"?

18

A NOTE ON BOARDING

Don't. Just don't. If you can afford to pay for overnight care while you're away, pay someone to do it *in your home*. Here's why:

- Any veterinarian worth a shit is going to tell you that animals do best in their own environments. Absenting yourself from that is disruption enough. Don't make it worse by tossing them into some unfamiliar space for days on end.
- Without fail, clients of mine who used boarding services reported their dogs were not themselves upon returning. They exhibited all manner of abnormal behaviors, from skittishness to lethargy to lack of appetite to digestive issues. Sometimes, this lasted days. Others, it lasted *weeks*.
- To make cleaning easier and reduce the likelihood of various incidental objects being destroyed, boarding

facilities are often an acoustic nightmare. Polished concrete floors, painted cinder block walls, no real furniture or any other surface that might absorb sound. Dogs have incredibly sensitive ears. Putting them in such a space for days on end, alongside other dogs barking, shrieking, and so on, is predictably stressful and anxiety inducing.

- The constant stimulation that such environments yield is similarly distressing. In the home, your little guy can curl up in a corner or some other secluded spot and have some alone time. This is rarely the case in daycare setups.

- I've had friends who've worked at boarding/daycare businesses. First, the turnover is constant. There are few barriers to entry for employment in these places, and the pay is such shit that people rarely stay long enough to develop any useful expertise. They're magnets for the terminally unhirable. And that's when businesses aren't simply finding some reason to shit-can people before the threshold of being legally obligated to provide benefits. Second, these friends have reported seeing dogs horribly mistreated—beaten with belts, in one particularly egregious case. This should be an *absolute* deal breaker. There's no excuse for this, and no meaningful way for you to insure against it, once the doors close.

Here's what you should do, instead:

- Find a freelance walker or pet sitter. Hiring an agency reduces your odds of having any rapport or direct relationship with the person caring for your animal.

- Ask for references. Contact said references. Any decent person in the trade should easily be able to provide you with three, and experienced ones can provide you with more. Neither should blink at this request. And yet, 90 percent of clients I met with *never asked.* Don't be surprised if the person you're asking won't give you phone numbers. That's a good sign, actually. You wouldn't want your pet sitter giving out *your* phone number, would you? E-mail their references, and ask *them* for their phone numbers, if you need to talk to a live person (talking to a live person is recommended).

- Once you've settled on someone, establish some quality controls. Solid pet sitters will offer to text you photos and brief notes about how things are going. It's 100 percent okay to request they do this. If they don't have a device capable of doing *both*, you've hired someone who either doesn't take their work seriously, or puts greater priority on some idiot principle about technology than they do your comfort. If you're on good terms with neighbors, put them in touch with your sitter, and have them check in once or twice. It'll add a layer of accountability, and provide a potential support in any unclear or emergency situation.

At the end of the day, direct relationships, community net-works, and the hard work of maintaining trust are better suited to ensuring the well-being of your companion animal. There is simply no substitute. Anyone who would tell you there *is* has some inter-est at stake to which your peace of mind will be subordinated, and should be kept at a great, great distance.

19

LITTLE DEATHS

The relative purposelessness of my movement throughout the day lacked the single-mindedness of the more traditional Point A to Point B jaunts, and that meant an atypical lack of distraction—and a mostly useless spectrum of detail present in any given moment. That lack of any driving narrative to my inner monologue meant *noticing*, which, for anyone in my line of sight, meant *being* noticed. It wasn't always a welcome shared experience.

Had it not been for the blanket wrapped around him, I might not have even given him a second thought. Deeply vulnerable, tender, even humiliating moments unfurl on people, indifferent to their preference of time and place, all day long. Breakups. Toddler meltdowns. Missteps and mild falls. Arrests. And the insidious, hushed secret of such contingency is that it is inversely proportionate to privilege. The homeless cannot hide how their bodies fail them, or the logical outcomes of scant access to toilets. Young black men are more likely to be cuffed on a curb in the afternoon sun than, for

instance, their landlords—despite the likely distribution of crimi-
nality between them. There's a decidedly not-accidental taxonomy
to people pleading into pay phones. And so on. Most of us spare
ourselves the ugly math of such constants, and thus surreptitiously
construct considerably less unsettling notions of the world we inhabit, by simply being indoors. Not even by choice. A fluency with
the equal parts structured and petty humiliations at hand in any
given moment—an intimacy with the attrition and moral indifference of each day's backstory is simply disciplined out of us by otherwise mundane demands on our attention.

I'd negotiated a tenuous peace with and an awkward etiquette
in being that not-altogether-willing witness to other people's personal moments. Opting for a deliberate state of distraction, ignoring people hit with some inopportune broadcast of their fallibility,
fear, or suffering in public space seemed a contribution to some
cosmic accumulation of cold human awfulness. I didn't want to
pass my day wandering about in that mind. So I settled for, in the
least invasive—often wholly nonverbal—manner I could conjure,
letting people know they weren't *alone* in the moments for which
they hadn't prepared. But often enough, being in the field, exposed
to whatever the human condition spit up in my presence, the cour-
tesy of allowing someone to believe they *weren't* seen was the most
gentle option, if not the most expedient. It was counterintuitive and
unsettling, but I learned to practice it as distinct from an aversive
reaction, with time and trial.

He'd launched out of the front entrance to his building with an unlikely urgency, like he was two steps behind something or someone critical to his day. Nineteenth and Florida NW. Given the hour, and the swelling density of telecommuters in those blocks, I figured he'd overslept, and bolted in the realization he'd missed some vital UPS delivery or such. Or perhaps he woke up sober and alone in the bed of someone he'd gone home with drunk, disoriented by the unfamiliar scenes around him. Regardless, despite his unsubtle, gesticulated panic, he seemed to go unnoticed by everyone but me.

But then he threw a curveball: he let the door close behind him. It threw me off. I tried and failed to read him, as he continued to wander Florida Avenue, his demeanor shifting into a sort of curiosity at his surroundings. Like he'd nodded off to snowfall, and woken to some *Twilight Zone* episode in which lower Adams Morgan sat brightening in the late-morning spring. He readjusted the blanket around his shoulders, pulling it tight at his chest, like he was settling into a more-than-momentary bout with the outdoor elements. Beneath his makeshift cloak, he wore nothing but a pair of bed shorts. Panic no longer registered. He wasn't locked out. Or if he was, he either didn't know or didn't care.

As an Alaskan husky and I ambled east on Florida, circling the block between Eighteenth and Nineteenth, I could see him at various points, wandering aimlessly. I watched him shuffling calmly at the base of Nineteenth Street's southward incline, back at the front of his building, observing traffic like it was utterly new to him. When we reached the intersection, he approached us.

"Do you know what time it is?" His voice lilted with an affect betraying his likely sexual orientation. Florida being the northern border of Dupont, it made sense. It was 2002. I wasn't carrying a cell phone, and I hated how watches felt, so I wasn't the best person for him to ask. The most I could do was guess based on what the kitchen clock read when I picked up the dog. "Ah, it's probably about 10:45."

Seeing him up close, his blonde hair curtained over what were more apparently sunken eyes. He was gaunt, though not otherwise visibly unhealthy. He pondered my answer in a manner befitting a disclosure of far greater consequence. I still half-suspected he was just pacing his building's entrance, awaiting something or someone's scheduled arrival.

"Say . . ."—he seemed to have forgotten our exchange up to that point, or simply lost interest—"Could you call me an ambulance?" I wanted to assure him this was a perfectly normal request; that he was still with the rest of us, out in the world. But it seemed unlikely I could adequately move through the task before me without further clarification, and the risk of flagging to him that nothing about his present situation made sense in the least.

"I don't have a phone on me, but when I take this dog home, I can call from there."

"That's fine," he said casually, returning his gaze to the passing cars.

His figure being what it was, his lacking any obvious signs of an emergency condition, and his seeming dissociation from even what he was asking left me wondering if he were living with late-stage AIDS; perhaps delirious from wasting, or mixing the wrong prescriptions.

"Can I tell them something in particular is wrong?"

"I just think . . . I think I'm *dying*."

In the shell of a once likely factory atop an EPA superfund site in Brooklyn, sometime in 2013, I watched the stories come so hurried and unrehearsed as to almost stumble over one another. A nineteen-year-old, newly sober. Anguished and enraged because everyone had told him it would be easier. And it wasn't. Nothing was easier. Everything was *awful*. No salvation was forthcoming, whatever his efforts. The two years that'd followed his parents kicking him out for his sexuality, he'd turned tricks to get by, and gotten high just to make it through each encounter. In short order, the dynamic flipped. Sex work serviced using. Staying clean and away from the johns blowing up his phone, while skipping meals and barely making rent. His speech was shaken. Full-bodied sobs.

Across from him, a man leaning into fifty described how using had been a salve for shame and stigma, as he eased into a life of any romantic or sexual possibility, after coming out; the only way to pry his way out of himself, and open to physical affection. Impaired, often risky affection. By the time he got clean, the two were fused, triggering one another. And in recovery, so were sobriety and celibacy. Seven years clean, confident he was better equipped than ever to forge healthy, rewarding romantic and sexual relations—*he couldn't.* The fear of relapsing was paralyzing. He was adjusting to the possibility that his survival may preclude intimacy; a sentence most would never have to ponder.

All firemen in the District are trained EMS, and given the distribution of firehouses, they're pretty much always the first responders. I wasn't surprised to see the fire engine clogging up Florida Avenue as I made my way to my next client. Two responders sat with him on the edge of a planting box, and I couldn't much tell what, if anything, they were doing. Toward the back of the truck, a guy who appeared to be the team's supervisor was radioing back to dispatch. I caught his attention.

"I'm the one who called it in. What happened?"

He shook his head and then shrugged, as if I were somehow knowing and in on his obvious, dismissive annoyance. "Meth." The easy answer.

A year or so later, we passed each other on that same block. He was fully clothed, this time, considerably more healthy looking. I searched his face for any sign he recognized me. He nodded a friendly hello. Perfect strangers.

20

MERRY CHRISTMAS: I HAD SEX IN YOUR HOUSE

The five-week period that runs from Thanksgiving to New Year's is *huge* for pet care. Especially the stretch running from Christmas Eve to the first days of January. While standard workday routes ebb during much of this period, requests for overnight care spike dramatically. Under the right circumstances, thousands of dollars can be made. You learn to take advantage of this fact. Schedule your family holiday to-dos mid-December, then take whatever you've banked from the season's work rush and go somewhere warm in February. Its effect on life routines is substantial, even annoying. But the payoff is often jaw dropping.

And typically some of this otherwise finite, episodic work can be converted into ongoing, daily clients. Someone hires you to care for or check in on their little ones while they're away, and they wind up liking you enough to keep you around. If you do the whole thing right, you should see your annual revenue increase substantially, year to year.

That said, this season is also *brutal*. The learning curve that comes with any new client relationship basically threatens everything, and with experience, that looming inevitability wears on the nerves. Often, the people who inquire about services during this window have never considered hiring someone to care for their pets, and every facet of what's material to the task is new to them. Alarm codes go unmentioned, and you wind up explaining to ADT (and usually the cops) why it is you're inside a home that doesn't match the address on your ID (or you just lock things back up and bail before they arrive). Leashes are hidden some place, and the client won't answer their phone. The dog that was perfectly friendly during the consultation is now defensive as fuck, and leashing them up involves ninja-level acrobatics (with good odds on comprising one's bodily integrity). So, in addition to the workload, you're managing contingency at pretty much every turn, with the added pressure of knowing that failure probably means someone rebooking a flight, to remedy whatever's come unhinged.

Obviously, once you've committed to staying overnight in someone's home, you can't then be booked to live out of someone else's. So you wind up working what I call *rounds*, from about 6 a.m. to just past midnight. Beginning with the dog(s) with which you're staying, you walk every dog you've booked (no matter the distances between them), as though they were yours. Morning. Midday. Afternoon. Dinner. Bedtime. Cats you're tasked with feeding get worked into that schedule, with less demanding frequency. Depending on how many clients you've taken on, these rounds can be three hours apiece, leaving maybe an hour between them.

This, in addition to commutes. I worked on a bike, and my rounds would often begin somewhere in central Capitol Hill, taking me as far east as RFK Stadium, then up to Trinidad, taking Florida Avenue (a pothole-laden gauntlet, wherein any cyclist is effectively disrupting every driver's personal make-believe music video—and tempting a corresponding rage) west across the District to Logan Circle, up the hill into Columbia Heights, Mt. Pleasant, Adams Morgan, and then finally back down to Dupont, before riding the four or five miles *back* to Capitol Hill.

We're also talking about late December, here. If I were lucky, precipitation wouldn't kick in until the new year. But often, I did rounds in the worst of winter weather. Snow. Freezing rain. "Wintry Mix" (on par with swarms of mosquitos, as experiences go). To survive, I layered like crazy, wore *two* cycling balaclavas simultaneously, and dropped $350 on a snowboarding jacket. I also acquired two pair of "slacks" made by a cycling company in Brooklyn, fashioned from material developed to prevent death from hypothermia in English airmen who survived being shot down over the channel in World War II. As soon as any liquid touched this fabric's surface, the threads swelled, fully sealing out moisture as though waterproof. I could actually pour coffee on them, and watch it bead up and roll off. These cost me $180 each. And they were (and remain) worth every goddamn penny.

One season, in addition to my own rounds (in a mix of light rain

and snow), I covered clients for another dog walker who'd booked
a full plate, but had to leave town for a family emergency. I did this
through the entire arc of a rather nasty flu, basically NyQuilling
myself into unconsciousness every moment I wasn't working—on
the *couch*, because climbing the stairs to the client's guest room
was implausible and merely put added yardage in play. The whole
process felt so unthinkable and ill advised that I actually kind of
relished the sheer lunacy of throwing myself into it, at each stage.
When it was over, I slept for three days straight.

It should come as no surprise that people laboring in such a capacity might avail themselves of all manner of relief and recreation
during downtime, even just to get out of their own heads. For most
of my peers, this probably involved drinking, weed, and so on. I
happen to be sober. My recreation mostly took the form of Chinese
delivery, *Arrested Development* marathons, and sex.

Before you get all scandalized about that last bit, let me just
say something for the record: if you hire someone to suspend their
normal life in order to live out of your house, with your companion animal, and you *don't* think they're going to do what people
always do with any nominal privacy . . . you're an idiot. Seriously.
That's primarily what homes are *for*. Most everything else can be
done elsewhere, with little risk or transgression, and if I learned
nothing else in my time keying in and out of them for a living, it's
that homes are primarily the enclosures in which people shit, fuck,
bleed, masturbate, and break.

Unlike guests, or even the odd workman or contractor, I encountered homes in all their candid vulnerability, day to day. When you woke up late, rushed into the shower, and left your skid-marked tighty-whities laying where you stepped out of them on the bathroom floor? *I saw them.* The note your girlfriend left you on the kitchen island, thanking you for the breakfast *and* the sex? I wasn't even trying to see it. The panties that suggested an ER–worthy hemorrhage that you left next to the bed, before your trip to your sister's wedding? I placed them on your dresser, using a pencil, out of your dog's reach. And then (using the same pencil) put them back where I found them an hour before you got back, so you could at least *hope* your modesty survived the weekend. The positive home pregnancy test your family didn't know about for another two to three months? I felt *so* special to be included in your secret. The iPad you left sitting next to the legal pad where you had me leave you notes about the walk? You had iMessage running, so I saw your prior night's booty call's half of your sexting session from the office, in real-time push notifications, as I let you know your puppy finally took a shit somewhere *other* than your living-room floor. The ten-item to-do list you'd made and left out before your business trip, which featured picking up dry-cleaning *and* having sex? I mostly wondered which end of the list suggested priority, and why—in either case—sex was number seven.

There's a passive voyeurism that comes with that sort of access. I didn't *want* to know these things about you. I certainly didn't *try* to. Sure, I had friends and girlfriends who snooped in your homes when they visited me. They found your weed, your giant dildos, your anal beads. They giggled like children, and invited me to join, and I declined. I actually had no desire to know more about you than you yourselves revealed; professionally, it seemed most prudent to allow you to drive that process, and be known on your own terms. And I guarded that delicate equilibrium quite studiously.

But seriously, you were terrible at keeping your own secrets, and worse—you advertised the parts of yourselves I'd have never expected you to. To this day, I wonder about a quirky young woman whose rescued pugs I walked for a year or so; a staffer for a somewhat tragically progressive congressman. Going in, it was clear she was new to dogs. But the more time I spent in her apartment, the more I wondered if she was just new to *life*. Each week, a new fad diet portioned out in individual Tupperware, meticulously stacked in the fridge. A college report card framed and hung in the hallway to the bathroom. Once, a stack of library books on the kitchen island, among them, *How to Have Conversations with People*.

Anyone in my position who cultivates condescension from such discoveries is a sociopath. And such people are likely, and sadly, abundant. These mishaps—these windows into the messy complexity of a life—are not scandalous, humiliating anomalies in a field of general and effortless grace. Rather, they are our common condition. They *are* the field. They lay bare our fallibility—and more importantly, our fragility—in ways that ought to appeal to instincts of mutual care and empathy. I can assure you, the world as reflected in the appearances we keep up, propelled by ego, career, or even higher pursuits . . . is a silly and childish facade. And it gives way to the worst in us, concealing what's softest, most humble, most compassionate.

So, to rage against the blunting of our best selves, and because we're all in this together—I fucked in your house. A *lot*. Like, every chance I got. If your neighbors didn't know you'd skipped town, they were probably really happy for you.

No need to thank me. Just doing my part.

21

THE PLAN, PT. 1 (THEIRS)

London's Stansted Airport was pretty bare bones in the fall of 2005. If you've ever traveled on one of Europe's budget airlines, you know its type. Typically, these facilities are well outside of the actual city to which they're attached, more so even than the major airports, and they offer little in the way of amenities. Tile floors, mesh-wire seating consoles, and, in this case, few actual walls. It was a fairly inhospitable place to find oneself overnight, and yet, it would be serving as my hotel room. After a brief tour through the UK with a band I'd been playing in, our drummer and I had flown to Sweden, spending a week between Stockholm and Umeå, visiting friends and attending the premiere of a documentary about the latter city's legendary hardcore band Refused. Stansted served as something of a hub for Ryanair, so we'd landed there on the back end of our trip, with a night to kill before my drummer friend grabbed an early-a.m. bus to a flight home out of Gatwick, and I continued on to visit a ladyfriend in Italy.

Neither of us being meat-eaters, we'd each procured a plate of greasy potatoes from the only food option in the building—a shitty diner near its center. The closing gates were coming down for the evening as we made our way to a table. Smartphones were only just getting around, wi-fi was not nearly as ubiquitous as it is now, and I'd read both of the books I'd brought during our drives in the UK. Having washed up and shaved in the airport bathroom, we were left with nothing but each other to pass the time.

He'd quit a job in a graduate-school library a few months prior, anticipating a month-long U.S. tour with his other band and then our trip across the Atlantic. This was how it went with musicians. You either had some sort of job you could come and go from with relative ease, or you strung stopgap work between tours, with no real trajectory or aim other than the ease of getting into a van every few months to run your life into the ground again. By this point, I'd quit working for dog-walking agencies, and had cultivated a fairly lucrative, stable freelance client base via Craigslist. I thus had a number of friends eager to sub for me when I wanted to travel. Many of them were dog walkers themselves, and the return on even a few weeks working my route was often worth quitting a job with an agency.

My drummer friend, on the other hand, was flying back to D.C. with no real prospects beyond groveling for some job he didn't want and wouldn't care about, which he'd quit six months later when his next tour kicked off. With the wee hours staring us down, I inquired as to his plans, and he more or less confirmed what anyone

familiar with the circumstances would've assumed. Despite leaving
Bates College with degrees in both literature and music, he'd likely
be temping. "Why don't you go work for a dog-walking agency?" I
asked. "It's a shorter workday, and once you can say you've done it,
you're always going to find someone willing to hire you." As it happened, my claim was borne out by institutional shifts afoot back in
D.C. More so, in fact, than either of us probably could've imagined.

Unlike every other city in the United States, the District of
Columbia exists as a sort of landlocked colony. While each of the
city's roughly 600,000 residents pays taxes to the federal government, they enjoy no representation within it. The federal government intervenes in the city's internal politics and administration
routinely, often at odds with the stated aspirations of its residents,
with precisely zero structural accountability. In its shadow, the District operated for many years as a near-failed state, especially since
the '68 riots. A feature-length *Frontline* special from 1990 depicted
people in the city's Shaw neighborhood living in conditions straight
out of apartheid South Africa; concrete shells of homes, with sheets
for doors. It was illustratively titled "Throwaway People." Remember the final shot in *Independence Day*; the multistory house with
the facade sheared off and the rooms exposed? That was an actual
structure near the corner of Fourth and Massachusetts NW, facing
a major city corridor, on the edge of D.C.'s Chinatown. It wasn't
staged for the movie. It stood exposed like that, a reminder to residents of their vulnerability, for what must've been decades. D.C.
would eventually—rather famously—be crowned the murder capi-

tal of the world, prompting the local NBA team to change its name
from the Bullets to the Wizards.

When I moved there in the mid-nineties, several public schools
couldn't open on time, due to gaping holes in the ceilings. Illiteracy
was widespread, and HIV/AIDS ravaged the population (coming
in as the eighth worst such epidemic in the world—the worst result in the Western Hemisphere, after Haiti). Understandably desperate to exact some triage in the havoc HIV had wrought on the
city, residents passed a number of referendums, with telling results.
The first of these (in my memory) was an initiative to establish a
publicly funded needle-exchange program. Lacking budgetary autonomy—a condition of which no other city in the United States
was left wanting—the funds for the program were withheld by the
U.S. Congress, and all near-term hopes for it collapsed. Another
was an effort to decriminalize medical marijuana, particularly for
residents living with full-blown AIDS, facing its latter stages—
"wasting syndrome": loss of appetite, chronic pain, and diarrhea
that leaves one practically withering away. The day of the referen-
dum, then Republican representative Bob Barr moved to *seize the
ballots* and have them locked away in a vault, before they could even
be counted. It took several years before a federal judge would order
them turned over and tallied. The Bush administration, in its typical, fanatical wisdom, barred all sex education that departed from
an abstinence-only model, with predictable, disastrous results in an
already battered, neglected youth population.

Some have argued that the city's overwhelmingly center-left to left politics account for the persistent refusal of the federal government to enfranchise its residents. Roughly 93 percent of the population votes Democrat, down the ticket, in every local election, and the local Green Party enjoys more support than the GOP. Were the District to be granted statehood, it would arguably amount to the most solidly left voting bloc in the country.

From my vantage point, as a fifteen-year resident of the city, D.C.'s disenfranchisement was about something far more insidious than partisan stonewalling. It was keenly racialized. For the latter half of the last century, D.C. was colloquially known as "Chocolate City"—at one point, its population was upward of 80 percent African American. (It's also home to the largest Ethiopian population outside the country itself.) Unlike other U.S. cities with comparable demographics, it is not subsumed within a majority-white state. And this makes it utterly (and gravely) unique. What no one seems to want to admit about the District's status within American democracy is what no white person wants to admit about the status of blackness in our culture: that it might speak for itself, in its own voice, cannot be tolerated. At any cost.

In the meantime, the city's suburbs in Maryland and Virginia have seen fit to forge a dizzyingly parasitic relationship with the whole arrangement. While the District is actually home to more jobs than people, two-thirds of the income earned in the city goes to nonresidents; people who utilize the city's public infrastructure, and capitalize on the vibrant, resilient economy driven by the presence of the federal government, but who don't pay for any of it. The income they earn in the District is taxed where they *live*—in Maryland and Virginia.

Montgomery County (Maryland) and Arlington County (Virginia) boast some of the highest-ranked public-school and library systems in the United States. Their fire, EMS, and police departments are similarly well regarded. The states themselves have robust, reputable public university systems, financed in no small part by the tax base pouring out of D.C. As a corrective to this extractive obscenity, the District has on multiple occasions sought to impose a commuter tax, or some system by which income *earned* in the city would be—to some extent—*taxed* in the city. And on each and every one of those occasions, the congressional representatives elected by the suburbs mobilized congress to deter, overturn, or neutralize the process. District residents, of course, have had no one to meaningfully intervene on their behalf. Ironically, as if to underscore the naked contempt the suburbs have for the city, District residents working in the suburbs have been obliged to pay taxes in both the District *and* whichever state they commute to for work.

The whole setup is so breathtakingly crass and, on its very face, predatory that lifelong, black District residents have sometimes resorted to making sense of it by way of a sort of folk myth known as "The Plan": basically, a superstition that a conspiracy exists to empty D.C. of black people. Ride a city bus, or shuffle about in the right corners of the District, and you're likely to hear mention of it. It's simple enough to wince at its cliché irrationality, but—quite sadly—there's a level at which it's not necessarily any more far-fetched or blunt-object than the reality on the ground.

At the time of our overnight stay at Stansted, Mayor Anthony Williams was two years into his final term, and practically untouchable, having followed on the heels of Marion Barry's post-prison return to the city's helm. Williams inaugurated his final stint announcing his intention to bring 100,000 new residents to the District within a decade. Despite the massive figure—and its proportion to the city's existing population, and the fact that it amounted to a reversal of the District's net decline in residents at that point—it wasn't an entirely implausible goal. Gentrification was fast afoot, and entire neighborhoods were being transformed almost overnight, with condo construction virtually everywhere, artificially inflating real-estate prices. Williams had no small role in enticing developers to the banquet, and his administration had undertaken a concerted rebranding campaign: "City Living, D.C. Style." In the end, it mostly succeeded. By 2013, data showed a net increase of 83,000 residents.

This came with predictable effects, not least because they were baked into Williams's strategy. He'd modeled the whole plan on a Brookings report titled *Envisioning a Future Washington*, drafted by a former chief of the District's financial control board. The report referred to something called "The Adult Strategy," which worked from the premise that an increase in high-earning, child-less residents would greatly increase the District's tax base. Higher incomes and higher property values = *greater tax base*. Textbook gentrification strategy. Nothing groundbreaking. Higher property values would yield higher tax obligations for existing, lower-income homeowners, and—even according to the report's own language— likely push them out "unless strenuous efforts were made to enable them to stay."

No metric was offered, however, for what sorts of efforts to retain low-income residents would qualify as "strenuous." In fact, the document was quite candid in projecting the impact such a plan would have on the city's racial demographics, noting it would "probably increase the ratio of whites to African Americans." That lack of subtlety pervaded the report's wording. "Long-time residents might fear that newcomers lacked lasting commitment to Washington," it warned, arguing such residents might *perceive* new residents as "[un]likely to fight for better schools or help for low-income families."

All of this, *while touting the District's cultural diversity as a draw*, and tacitly suggesting former and downsized psychiatric and homeless facilities could be repurposed for commercial or residential development. In effect, inasmuch as racially and culturally diverse communities served as marketing fodder, they were a critical piece of the proposed vision. Once that vision was set in motion, however, said communities would be scattered to the wind, their cries little more than an ethereal "perception problem."

Then, there was the "childless" bit, which struck me as positively *breathtaking*. When Mayor Williams announced this plan, I remember wondering aloud whether it was the first time in U.S.

history that an elected politician had gone on record with an *anti-family* policy proposal. The obvious—and rather nakedly cynical—play being made was that children were a tax burden. They had to be educated, and provided for via public coffers in other myriad ways. The bait and switch implied by this strategy was: if the city is remade to lure twenty- and thirty-somethings, it will continue to draw them. When they have children, and the city's orientation and priorities no longer prove accommodating, they'll leave. At which point, *new* single residents will replace them.

In effect, the strategy appeared to grow the city's tax base (mostly) by reducing its obligations (to children). If the District's unique tax-base challenges were viewed as analogous to a critical economic downturn (and the report devoted considerable space to setting it up in almost exactly this way), this was little more than what corporations would call an asset-based recovery; downsize, do more with fewer people, and never bring back the workers cut loose.

(Of course, the report's *second* prong was "The Family Strategy: More Middle-Income Families with Children." Looking at its specifics, it's hard not to conclude it was merely a public relations consideration. In contrast with the "childless" strategy, its requirements were abstract and far more heavily weighted toward nebulous obligations to be borne by "the community." The mechanisms proposed to ensure this strategy's viability indicated no clear metrics.)

The outcomes were predictable. As was the explosion in demand for pet care that came with all the new "childless" households.

22

THE PLAN, PT. 2 (OURS)

Six months out from Stansted, our hosts from Umeå had taken up in my house for the last leg of winter. One on my couch, one in my bed. More than a year had blown by since I'd been forced to give up on my marriage, and despite some travel and a number of material upgrades, the life I woke up to each day still proved unfamiliar— and mostly unengaging. It wasn't *sad*; it just wasn't what I'd spent the better part of a decade growing into, and still mostly felt like a consolation prize for which I had no real affection or passion.

Treading water like that had grown so bleak and, more so, *boring* that I'd decided to check out and pursue something adventurous for its own sake, just to disrupt the tedium. A bike messenger in Stockholm had talked me into plotting a series of low-elevation rides around Sweden at the end of summer. Factoring in downtime visiting with friends in various cities, I'd budgeted that I'd need a few grand, and a few months. At the beginning of the year, I told one client to stop paying me and just set aside whatever I had due;

it functioned as a savings account I could put out of mind, and by the time I got on the plane, I'd have way more than necessary for the two months I'd staked out. My houseguests had offered to carry back a wheel set my coconspirator asked to buy off me, but before they'd even left, he'd backed out of it, and I got spooked he might bail on the whole plan, potentially sticking me with the expense of flights I thankfully hadn't booked, yet. My adventure quickly withered on the vine.

Meanwhile, my drummer friend *had* gone and gotten himself hired at a dog-walking agency. He said it suited him for the time, but he wasn't committed to it beyond his band's next tour, which happened to be ending right when I was planning on skipping town. It wasn't hard to convince him to sublet my house, and cover my clients for two months. I just had to figure out where to *go*.

I decided on Montpelier, Vermont. There was a small, intellectually vibrant crew of anarchists I'd befriended there, who mostly drew from the tradition Murray Bookchin had established through the Institute for Social Ecology. Unlike most places in the United States, Vermont was still governed via face-to-face assemblies, with elected leaders carrying out decisions ratified from below. The first articles of impeachment against Dick Cheney following the Iraq invasion were submitted by Vermont senator Patrick Leahy. Likely begrudgingly, but he wasn't given a choice: it had been decided in the local assemblies.

It wasn't just structural. It was an *attitude*. Beyond Vermont's reputed progressive streak—which itself was far more complicated than typically acknowledged—was a certain democratic zeitgeist. The legacy of Italian anarchist immigrants who once worked as stonecutters in the region was apparent in various markers; an anarchist and socialist labor hall still holds events in Barre, just over from the capitol. My friends there had recently opened a small, volunteer bookstore upstairs from a worker-run café in the center of Montpelier, and invited me to do shifts there while in town. Compared to D.C., August and September that far north are gloriously forgiving, rent was cheap, and two months of biking, skinny-dipping, and coffee seemed preferable to my sleepwalk in D.C. I found a short-term apartment through a friend and booked a flight.

March became April. Then May. The prospect of my impending northward retreat had done little to blunt my restlessness. As my escape drew closer, it became more material, less abstract—and thus less ripe with possibility. The odds were I'd come right back to the same comfortable-yet-unenchanting rut, which made the whole thing seem pointless and naïve. I had hit a sort of ceiling. I owned my labor, I was comfortable, and inasmuch as there was only so much work I could take on, there wasn't much of anything to be ambitious about, professionally. Most of the activist work I'd been part of had either grown prohibitively toxic or emotionally unhealthy. Much of it had imploded, and what was left seemed likely to meet the same fate. The most rewarding and dynamic group of organizers I'd worked with had slowly and amicably dispersed by way of graduate studies, sabbaticals, newborns, and other mundane life transitions. I'd settled on doing childcare for a local anti-gentrification project, just to be involved in *something*.

I don't remember exactly when it started, but an idea began percolating, and I spent each of my workdays for a full week turning it over and over. I knew dog walking inside and out, top to bottom. I'd seen what past employers had botched, and how existing models underserved both workers and clients. My friend's time covering my clients for August and September could serve as an apprenticeship. Upon my return from Vermont, we could split my work into two routes, and run the work as a team. When the workload grew sufficiently, we could expand the project to a third person. And so on. Scaled this way, we could share a health-insurance policy, organize our work on a directly democratic model, cover each other's work where necessary—for sick days or nonremunerative passions—without anyone having to quit their job, and to the extent the project succeeded and grew, it would provide that opportunity and freedom to greater numbers of people. The operating overhead and margins being what they were, the clients themselves served as startup capital; most initial outlays could be cash flowed. We'd turn our day job into both a means of day-to-day self-determination, and a living, breathing demonstration of anarchist self-organization.

Saturday morning, I put it all down into a Jerry Maguire–esque e-mail to my drummer friend—knowing full well my enthusiasm likely exceeded his. Hitting send took deep breaths. Once irretrievable, I felt the dread of adolescent romance and the embarrassment of having overread and overreached. Sometime that afternoon, stricken with shame at my overactive imagination, I called.

"So I sent you this e-mail. It's a bit over the top."

"I know. I saw it. It's really unsettling how alike we are in our thinking."

I spent my shifts at the bookstore in Montpelier researching incorporation options, liability insurance, and drafting website content. We each kicked in five hundred dollars for the minimum balance on a business checking account, and put our first year's professional association and liability premiums on a credit card—paid off in a month. A graphic designer I'd been on a few dates with put us through some pretty challenging, demanding conversations about branding, resulting in a downright *incredible* logo and a solid set of guiding principles for merging our presentation as a service and a political project. And we committed ourselves to putting our workplace—and its stability as a low-overhead operation—in the service of an unapologetic and uncompromising political vision, both in what we did and did not do, and where we collaborated with peers to allocate available material resources.

Somewhat firmly, we constructed our workplace around a number of foundational principles:

- Consensus democracy within our workplace. This, in contrast with the familiar, majoritarian forms of voting. We all had to agree to a decision, and decisions about which someone felt exceptional opposition could be blocked, entirely. Seniority, alliances, and other factors corrosive to democracy were ruled out, from the jump.

- Generous paid time off, particularly for artistic or political passions. Livelihoods exist to serve us, not the other way around. They should sustain and encourage the parts of us that enrich and fulfill us, as people. Further, they should *value* those parts of us such that they structurally ensure their flourishing. We began with one month each, annually. We added a week each successive year.

- Worker-ownership, and—within a year of launching—a communized pay scale. This meant that we were paid as members of the collective, not by the volume of labor we performed. Initially, this simply made calculating vacation pay easier, and resolved the issue of new collective members being stuck working newer, less-developed routes with sometimes only a few invoices and little pay, while others worked far more lucrative routes.

But it wound up really opening up questions of value, and how a given worker's contribution to the creation of that value is calculated. If someone walking dogs on a route spanning three adjacent neighborhoods was forced to cover a new client from an outlier neighborhood (perhaps a neighborhood we wanted to break into), it put his or her quality of service at risk and strained their time management. This could've actually resulted in *lost* clients, if service was compromised. Thus, the value of someone working even that *one* outlier client could not be pegged to the value of that client's invoice; that foothold represented revenue from future clients in that neighborhood, but also the value lost in comprising the quality of another worker's performance, should they have to stretch themselves.

This was a central debate in anarchist-communism, going back more than a hundred years, actually. Given the value contributed by innovations, new tools, and methods, not to mention differing *abilities* (especially sheer physical abilities), the metrics by which a given worker's earnings are calculated are fairly arbitrary. They typically reflect altogether other considerations— pitting workers against each other in competitive arrangements whose benefits accrue well above them, for instance. Further, cleaving the calculation off from larger social forces is disingenuous (access to education, class, gender, etc.). Rather than foster an environment or ethic of competition, we set ourselves up to privilege mutual aid and support. It saved our asses in more than a few critical situations.

- Work distribution was organized by neighborhood (and clusters of neighborhoods), so that all work could be conducted via bike or public transit. The carbon footprint of this approach was less interesting to us than the fact that it had prefigurative, propaganda value: why are the services we use organized the way they are? Might they be organized otherwise? Our clients were put face to face with this, each time they engaged with us.

- Health care. Most of us had spent our entire adult lives without it, and functioning as a workplace, rather than isolated freelancing agents, allowed us to both negotiate a solid plan at lower costs, and socialize the costs between us. For instance, the women in our workplace were assigned twice the premiums of men, by insurers. To rectify this, we divided the lump sum of all the premiums, and deducted their costs equally from the collective members on the company health policy.
- An explicit politics. We were clear about who we were, and what we stood for. And wherever possible, we sought to make that irresistibly relatable.

We started with roughly $30,000 annually in clients I'd cultivated while freelancing, in November of 2006. Our first full year up and running, we multiplied that figure several times over. The following year, we did the same. Bands went on tour. Bike trips on far coasts were taken. Growing pains were endured. And quality of life improved for all of us. On *our* terms.

23

PUG LIFE

"So, this is Dov and Tzippi," Dougie said, making my acquaintance with two ridiculous-looking, geriatric pugs as we eased into a third-floor condo half a block off Embassy Row. When he paused to consider possible introductory details, I cast furtive glances at distant corners of the apartment, the inhabitants of which seemed to occupy a higher tax bracket than god himself. Tzippi barked at me indignantly for shifting my attention, her tongue wagging sideways through a gap where several teeth used to be. Freestanding stairs zigzagged from the space where the dining and living rooms met, leading to what I'd assumed was a lofted master bedroom. Stretching onto my toes, I could see that the elevated area was, in fact, a whole other floor, with stairs at the back leading to a third. Trying not to give away my absolute shock, I silently noted the extravagance, given what was effectively a penthouse unit in a not altogether modern building.

At the far end of the living room was a giant bay window looking out across Twentieth Street NW onto the Indonesian Embassy. Even from our vantage point, I could make out the residual red stain on the embassy steps, dating back some years, to when friends had pelted the entrance with paint-filled balloons as the Suharto regime wiped out a quarter of the population of East Timor. Such were the more traditional circumstances of my "business" in this corner of the District. I gazed down, feeling something of a stowaway. Dougie was getting out of the proverbial game. He was moving on to take astrology classes or study Jungian dream interpretation or something. I honestly don't remember—it may have been *both*, knowing him. His next steps were less pressing for me than the fact that his clients represented some $50,000 annually, and he was handing them off to our fledgling worker-owned agency.

The increase would allow us to build internal capacity to establish routes in neighborhoods where we only had a handful of outlier clients, as well as accelerate material support we'd begun providing for social-movement work that our peers were doing. During my time freelancing, I'd lucked into a barter arrangement in which I did daily walks that covered half my rent on a small house on the east side of Capitol Hill, owned by an anarchist professor I knew with roots in anti-Apartheid and Palestine solidarity struggles. When I moved out a few years later, rather than renegotiate the arrangement, I invited him to donate what I'd have billed him each month to the Institute for Anarchist Studies—an outfit that gave grants, as well as editorial and publication support, to movement writers, historians, and other movement knowledge producers who lacked access to the funding on offer in the academic world. We'd both been board members there, and thus knew the value of the work they were doing. By mentally removing just *one* client from my "books" in a sort of tithe, roughly $5,000 a year was now going to the project.

At which point a lightbulb went on for me. I had spent years watching grassroots efforts either hobble into eventual collapse—underresourced and thus strategically adrift—or blunt their potential at the altar of institutional funding or NGO affiliation. But as a collective—with an overt politics present in how we organized our work—we'd be able to approach this in a new way. We were suddenly in a position to funnel otherwise unlikely sums to projects that would have seemed unpalatable to more timid sources of funding. Many noble projects weren't the kind of thing that offered a tax write-off, and we could compensate.

The conditions we laid out were deliberately concise: any project we funded had to be local, and in need of support for a particular task. Part of this was strictly pragmatic. We wanted our friends and allies in local struggles to set real goals, even if the achievement of a given goal had lackluster results. At the very least, it meant that the projects we were backing were willing to learn from pushing themselves into new ways of doing things. That entailed measurable progress for movement work, even if the gains were less material.

We also suspected that the example we were elaborating day to day might be replicated—improved upon, even—by peers in other cities, or other trades. Both our internal model and our relationship to organizing work suggested real potential for acquiring the means of production in low-capital enterprises, and leveraging those spaces as proof of concept *and* mutual aid. If that example was to be taken up by others, we wanted to emphasize the priority of local struggles. Beyond that, the people doing a lot of the work we supported knew that work best. Their autonomy was of a premium to us, so we stayed out of their way.

Amid all this, we were also adapting to the pace of being in business—a pace that, quite frankly, took us entirely by surprise. The brother of an organizer I knew was part of a collective in Canada, providing web development and general web strategy services. It turned out he was a fucking *genius*. He'd taken us on with a contract we paid monthly, building our site using Joomla (a competitor to Drupal), which allowed us to update and manage things through a web interface. Further, he applied search-engine optimization to the site, managed our Google AdWords account, and provided monthly statistics and recommendations for maximizing what we got out of it all. The effect was *enormous*. At one point, at his suggestion, we encouraged clients who were already using services like Yelp to review us. The first three that were posted bumped our Google ranking such that, in one day, we received ten client inquiries—a record. From that, we locked in new clients worth an annual gross of $60,000. Basically, in a single day, without warning, we all got a 20 percent raise.

At the time, applying such tools to dog walking appeared to

be relatively unheard of (in D.C., anyway), and our little band of anarchists began to dominate the relevant web searches. We were fielding new inquiries daily, locking most of them down by routing them through a form on our site linked to an e-mail alias, which was pointed at an actual collective member's e-mail. By collective policy, inquiring clients had to receive a reply within ten to fifteen minutes, with a signature file indicating the reply had been sent via smartphone. Straight out of the gate, this performed responsiveness to potential clients, and made it apparent we were equipped to handle last-minute details from the field, in real-time—that this was conveyed not by a sales pitch, but via the client's own *deduction* only made it more convincing. In a care trade, the value of it happening that way was incalculable.

The web form required clients to provide their nearest cross streets, so our initial reply would notify them whether they were in our service areas, and (if so) which of our collective members would be their primary walker. This communicated that, if they hired us, they'd be in a *direct* relationship with the person holding their keys and walking their dog, and that the collective—rather than being a management go-between for a rotating cast of anonymous walkers—served to ensure the client's interests should their primary point person perform poorly. Before an inquiring client even got a reply, their designated collective member would be forwarded their request, at which point that person had twenty-four hours to contact the client to schedule a consultation. Even gaming search-engine algorithms, in most cases we were one service among any number that a potential client contacted. Through this protocol, we'd often instilled confidence in and scheduled a consultation with a client before other agencies had even read their inquiry.

The number listed on our website was pointed at my phone more often than not, so I had a pretty direct interface with how people reacted to what we were doing. It wasn't uncommon for someone to call, kind of flustered, and say "I just forewent *The Washington Post* this morning, and read your entire website, instead." While explaining services and pricing, I'd also inform clients that we ran the company democratically, and that each of us had access to full health benefits and six weeks of fully paid vacation annually—something no other agency could say. Ninety percent of the time, the person I was talking to would pause, before coming back with something like, "Jesus. Can I come work for you?" I never really got over that. Lawyers. Congressional staffers. City employees. Doctors. Federal employees. All asking if they could come join an anarchist operation.

One day before starting work, I returned from the shower to a voicemail from the owner of a conventional, top-down agency, seemingly beside himself in awe, lavishing us with praise. "I've never seen anything like this." Listening, I kept waiting for him to make some proposal, to *want* something—to sell us his clients, or some referral arrangement, or some cross promotion. This happened from time to time; business owners were always trying to negotiate some new edge, or a parachute out of actually *working*. Weirdly, the voicemail ended without him doing anything of the sort. Either he just called to tell us he loved us, or he got so caught up in what he was saying that he forgot to make his pitch.

All of this had, I'm convinced, very little to do with any singular genius on our part, so much as a generalized dissatisfaction—despair may have even been more accurate. Even people who appeared to have jumped through every hoop on the road to "stability" seemed exhausted—and those were the lucky ones, who hadn't been saddled with extraordinary levels of debt just to get there. I sat in a café behind the Securities and Exchange Commission one afternoon, eavesdropping on a woman roughly my age interviewing for a position in some or another political campaign. As she rattled off her experience, I visualized it in a timeline. She had never actually *lived*. Never had a chance. From high school, to undergrad, to internship, to grad school, to internship, to campaign, to campaign, to staff position, to campaign—and on and on. I honestly had difficulty figuring out when she *slept*, given how she described the workdays she'd kept up in these gigs. And this was a young woman whose parents had every reason to be over the moon at her success; someone headhunted by campaign directors for her apparent skill and stamina. To what end, exactly? And what other option did she have, anyway?

Tzippi and Dov's companions, as Dougie explained that day, were a gay couple that spent roughly $180 a week to have him coax their senile, increasingly feeble—albeit adorable—would-be children half a block to the Gandhi statue opposite the Phillips Collection, twice daily. This, when the dogs were not residing at their *other*—far more modest—home on the far side of the historic gay-borhood, in a shared custody arrangement with a repartnered ex. The wealthier of the couples tended to cover the expense of the walks, regardless of where the dogs were housed—either out of some goodwill, or just an affinity for conspicuous consumption. Eventually, one of the two better-off gentlemen would confess to me that he commuted to New York by plane three times a week, where he worked for a Wall Street law firm representing a major financial firm in bankruptcy. The other made partner at a K Street firm after representing Enron in the class-action suit brought against them following their eponymous collapse.

At least that's what it said on the framed event program mounted on the wall of the room some architect had almost certainly intended as a guest bedroom with a full bath, but which was now lovingly converted into a sort of daytime barn-stable for two small, aging dogs; daily decorated and redecorated with their errant excrement.

This extravagance was the backdrop for the more or less total evisceration of every meritocratic trope that had been beaten into me, growing up. At this point, I no longer had many illusions about the upward distribution of wealth that drives the bulk of human activity. What was new was the license I felt to dispense with equivocation as to the moral questions embedded in that the idea of meritocracy—not merely the morality of capitalism's distributive outcomes, but the sorts of behavior it incentivizes, and the unflattering lie it gives to our collective identity.

As I carried the dogs to the triangle of grass spilling out around the Mahatma each day (it steadily proved less work than trying to make them walk), I'd sometimes replay my mother's lectures to me about initiative, education, and work ethic. Often enough, these had amounted to a nod in the direction of some poor soul, and a "Study hard, or you'll end up like him"—a (rather common) parental tactic less emphatic about the value of education than it was disdainful of poor people. I'd imagine her or some teacher saying, "Work hard, go to bat shielding monsters from accountability for the havoc they wreak in others' lives . . . and you, too, might be able to make some portion of a gazillion-dollar apartment smell like an outhouse!" It wasn't enough that incomprehensible rewards were showered on those who legally enabled the avaricious to shit all over untold numbers of people. Those rewards were, themselves, so abundant and apparently expendable that they could (quite literally) be shit all over, as well.

Steinbeck is famously quoted saying that the reason socialism never took root in the United States is that no American believes they are working-class; we're simply all "temporarily embarrassed millionaires." We are *not* millionaires, in any sense. We are, rather, as a whole impoverished in every meaningful way. I'm not altogether convinced we're embarrassed, either. It's not necessary to cite all the various statistics about wealth disparities and the force with which they bludgeon the human condition. It's enough to look at what wealth—and the drive for it—has made of us; its implicit morality; that today, tomorrow, or the next day, a child in south Lebanon will

be cut in half by a toy-looking object left in a field, *actually* an un-
exploded cluster bomb someone at Lockheed got *very* rich selling
to the Pentagon. Ultimately, the pipeline by which reward flows to
the insidious is—apparent in the sheer volume it conducts—vast.
And the monuments erected to it in the lives of those so rewarded,
at best, reflect a stunning lack of self-awareness. At worst, they're
obscene. The vector by which fortune accrues to those with even
a modicum of concern for anyone or anything but themselves is
what we colloquially refer to as *coincidence*. There exists no metric
by which we can claim to value the only thing that actually matters
in this life: *being gentle*. It is conditioned out of us, maligned, and
mocked in any case where it might matter, and then paraded about
with a cynical lack of irony, as if anyone powerful enough to conduct such spectacles gave the faintest fuck.

Whatever its successes, our little collective had simply managed
to game a very small corner of this bad joke, and we were keenly
aware that such gaming was not, on its own, any sort of redemptive
or sufficient condition.

None of which is to suggest that I didn't see the compassion in
devoting such resources to the care of two very old dogs—nor is it
fair to say that these men were, in their personalities, contempt-
ible. Hardly. They were incredibly kind, personable, and generous
toward me. But such is the banality of evil, no? I wasn't being asked
to perform any task ethically prohibitive in and of itself. The crucible in which our collision occurred was keenly compartmentalized;
simple and comfortable enough to eclipse the barbarity it neces-
sitated, though perhaps not its own absurdity. I'd still encounter

Salvadoran women who'd dragged themselves across the border, fleeing United States–funded bloodshed and civil war, and now scraped some threadbare living, keying into the penthouse week to week, to clean up after the whole sad comedy. And this was a world we'd all somehow tacitly agreed to live in—one in which we somehow didn't share any notable bewilderment or embarrassment.

"You know," Dougie said, clearly amused. "These dogs were Bar Mitzvah'd."

"Get the fuck out of here," I shot back. Even as comedy, it didn't seem plausible.

"I'm not kidding!" he insisted, becoming slightly more serious. "When they turned thirteen, Zack went to his rabbi, and said he wanted to have it done, and the guy apparently flat out refused. So he told him that was a shame; he'd planned to leave the temple a million dollars in his will."

Dougie seemed disappointed in my lack of response. The truth was that I had no words. Wills were as abstract to me as anything counted in millions. The joining of the two in a single sentence, with regard to someone in whose home I happened to be standing, honestly stunned me.

Frustrated, Dougie resumed, as if rounding out a joke that'd have typically involved a cast of clerics in a brothel or a space shuttle. "So the rabbi says, 'You didn't tell me they were Jewish!'"

In what felt like a silence of almost tragic weight, I ran my hands over my face, wincing in a "this is why we can't have nice things" moment of resignation. "All right, then. What's the routine, here?"

24

OMAR

*What strikes me is the fact that in our society, art has
become something which is related only to objects and not
to individuals, or to life. That art is something which is
specialized or which is done by experts who are artists. But
couldn't everyone's life become a work of art? Why should the
lamp or the house be an art object, but not our life?*

—*Michel Foucault*

Since "retiring" from dog walking, I've spent most of my time in
transit, living out of an oversize messenger bag in various corners of
the world. I find it, on the whole, far less aggravating than sedentary
life, for reasons that may seem (at first, anyway) counterintuitive.
I've found that fluency with one's conditions inclines one toward
second-guessing circumstances that are better just observed and
accepted. To have specific expectations of a situation is to be unable
to meet contingency with any skill or flexibility—it begets an ugly
sort of arrogance. Moving through experience with even a subtle

sense of entitlement to routine, predictability, explanation, and so on is—in addition to being unchallenging—incredibly stressful. When I'm on a subway car in New York, stopped between stations as happens with some regularity, my inner monologue quickly, and without any real effort, shifts into "It's not supposed to be this way." That utterance implies another: that things are *supposed* to be some other way. This impulse, while subtle, establishes a baseline in one's life mostly at odds with ease.

A lack of familiarity with one's circumstances or surroundings disables such sensitivities, at least after some time. One doesn't *know* how things are "supposed" to be, in such scenarios. One (hopefully) has no entitlements, as an outsider. Which is not to suggest that one ought to go blindly or naively into situations of real risk. There's simply a difference between caring for oneself and one's well-being, and putting demands on the world that are pointless and wildly lacking in perspective. Granted, it's perfectly practicable to be less attached to preferences in one's *own* environment. The opportunities are, at least on the surface, simply less abundant, or perhaps just less obvious. Our environments are simply not structured for us to notice such things, and we're trained to approach life—especially particular facets of it—in ways that treat anything nonnormative as an obstacle or even a net loss.

Unless we decide that they're not.

Some of the clients Dougie had handed off to our collective at the beginning of 2007 lived in a luxury condo building just south of Logan Circle, one of many that characterized the rapid transformation of just about everything east of Sixteenth Street NW. With this "luxury" motif came certain touches aimed less at any substantive improvement in anyone's quality of life, and more a matter of what I guess could be called showmanship; a psychological ROI for those who'd bought into the whole narrative of D.C. living, *remade*. The front of this particular building's lobby had a vaulted ceiling that climbed past the second floor, with glass window panels looking out onto Thirteenth Street NW extending up from the entrance. The inside was outfitted with a lighting system rigged to what I surmised was some sort of thermometer, softly coloring the adjacent walls to signal outdoor temperatures to residents exiting the building. How this was of any use to anyone who'd already ventured out of their apartment, down the elevator, and into the lobby, I have no clue. But according to some real-estate developer, it's value-added to have your building's lobby tell you whether or not you're dressed poorly, once it's mostly too late to do anything about it.

Another feature of this particular building was that, initially anyway, it didn't allow dog walkers to hold keys to residents' units— or even to the building. On the surface, this could be passed off as a more rigorous approach to security. But given how many people's keys I held day to day—and the nonexistent impact that'd had on anyone's home security—it was a bullshit measure. Its function was performative and pretentious. To access clients' homes, I had to be buzzed into the building by the concierge and have him accompany me to each unit to key me in. The same was true when *returning* dogs to their homes. Predictably, this was time consuming, some

days more than others. I would *race* UPS guys to the door, knowing
full well they came with a pushcart full of delays; contractors and
cleaners, for their part, typically posed an absolute clusterfuck. Half
the time, they'd arrived well before me, and I was left pacing the
lobby while some fuckup of theirs was remedied.

The concierge at this building happened to be a very sweet,
exceedingly kind Egyptian man, justifiably beloved by everyone
living there. He was also a devout Muslim. This meant he prayed
five times daily, suspending all functions for which his participa-
tion was required. I had late-morning *and* afternoon walks, in the
building. The odds of our respective, appointed obligations colliding were generally pretty good. It was not infrequent that I found
myself standing outside the main entrance, with and without dogs,
waiting for him to finish his prayers, so I could get buzzed in.

There was also the matter of his having to accompany me in the
task of managing dogs, at all, given they were deemed unclean by
the interpretation of Islam to which he was partial, and any contact with them whatsoever would require him to bathe head to toe
before praying again. This posed a demanding and considerable lo-
gistical challenge. A dog that's heard the telltale sounds of an impending walk is typically at the door, on the verge of jumping out
of its own skin. Totally unpredictable in its movements. Getting between them and the guy who'd just opened the door with sufficient
speed and agility to prevent a rather likely collision of the two, is
what one might call a nonstandard trade skill. Locating a leash that
may or may not be immediately visible—in order to stabilize the

situation—added another level of difficulty. I often hobbled around apartments hunched over, holding a dog's collar while in search of their leash, just to head off catastrophe.

Then there was the (often excited, erratic) walk back to the elevator, and the importance of maintaining a no-contact buffer zone within its confines, the whole ride down.

Some of the coworkers who subbed for me on occasion were vocal about *loathing* this whole process, often in dismissive remarks bordering on Islamophobic. "Fucking Omar and his fucking prayers. If you've gotta do that shit, you shouldn't take that job." To my knowledge, no one was ever anything but kind to him, but I never really understood how they rationalized their frustration.

In his short book, *On the Shores of Politics*, the French philosopher Jacques Rancière articulates a particular characterization of equality; a departure from conventional, typically *liberal* notions of equality. For Rancière, equality is not a *condition*—it's not a state of being that we bring about through this or that measure. Rather, in his analysis, equality is a *practice*; a potentially counterfactual assumption that *everyone*—regardless of race, class, gender, nationality, or any other such consideration—is equally capable of making meaningful decisions about their lives. More still, for Rancière, a (small *d*) democratic politics cannot even get off the ground without our taking up and committing to this practice, moment to moment. At its core, this means beginning from a position of taking people seriously, *as people*, and not putting conditions on our willingness to do so. The measure of equality, for Rancière, is the degree to which we *begin* from this practice.

Buddhist practitioners are routinely instructed to experiment with going through a day imagining that everyone but *them* is enlightened, and that everything that happens in their day—every conversation, every encounter, every snag, every joy—is designed to bring about their own enlightenment. There's no morality to it; it's simply intended to produce a nonhabituated reading of one's experience. Its function is simply experimental.

When my high-school art teacher introduced us to cubism, she described cubist works as portraits that functioned as though painted onto a Rubik's Cube, then turned in various sections, and represented in two dimensions. For whatever reason, it unlocked something for me. I looked at Picasso's works in a totally different way, able to see how what was effectively a disruption applied to established method had yielded extraordinary, inexplicably captivating images. Works that were *not possible* otherwise.

Omar's prayer schedule and all it demanded of him was that twist in the portrait that was my workday. It was a constraint that— as all constraints do—had productive effects. It forced me to improvise and innovate in how I went about my work routines. It forced me to be *curious*. It was the running of a completely different obstacle course; a prompt for the cultivation of different forms of knowledge, different skillsets. *Outside* my habituated routine.

More still, my mastering the routine it set up served to accommodate and normalize *difference*. It served to make other ways of living more possible. Not just for him. For me. That had the effect of making the general ecosystem in which I lived and worked measurably more conducive to people's *freedom*. In real, tangible terms. I can't imagine that being uninteresting. I can't imagine it *not* being absolutely invigorating.

I can't imagine it being anything but utterly necessary, required reading. I was grateful for it, every time I showed up.

25

EXPIRATION DATES

I'd watched his building go up over the course of about a year, one of a handful in the neighborhood planting the flag of eastward gentrification. Its layout was maze-like, the route to his unit running the length of several impractically carpeted hallways from the elevator, broken by a corner roughly midway. At the consultation, I discovered just how significant and harrowing that stretch would prove. His dog, Jimmy, was *ancient*. Deaf, nearly blind, barely able to stand. Getting the poor guy outside, day to day, was like walking a coffee table, and I was white knuckled with terror that he'd empty himself in one manner or another somewhere between his door and the elevator. Jimmy clearly *loathed* being dragged out each day. Worse, he seemed painfully bewildered by the whole process, each new excursion seeming to underscore his having forgotten the last one. I felt like an orderly, hauling some senile old man out of his home, for a routine that had negligibly little to do with his comfort or well-being.

This was the unsettling dilemma I found buried in so many of these encounters. It wasn't about Jimmy or his needs. It was about the client's, and the symbiosis of human-animal relationships. And the human half invariably dominated. The dogs gave few fucks about when I showed up, in most cases, but humans absolutely panicked. Dogs mostly loved absolutely everyone, and yet consultations almost always involved a client projecting onto me some particularly compelling "connection." I lost count of how many times one of the dogs rolled around in something dead during a walk, but I know exactly how many times I informed a client their guy or gal was rubbing it all over their apartment: *zero*.

That delicate dance with human emotional needs proved a trial by fire, really. The process was never just mediated by my relationship with a dog, or my rapport with a given client. I had keys to these people's homes. I knew their partners, in many cases; saw those relationships ebb and flow. I knew where they visited their families, where they vacationed for anniversaries. I saw them sick, injured, laid off from their jobs, grieving loved ones. Once, I was struck by a car while biking to a client's house; I took out the rear passenger window with my lower back, leaving ugly glass lacerations at the point of impact (which were later *glued* shut in an ER). The client raced home from work to clean my wounds and bandage me up. There was often a real intimacy coursing through the various relationships I had with these people, and even where there wasn't, I had an incidental, disproportionate knowledge of their lives that acted on our dynamic, whether I wanted it to or not.

I nonetheless felt some accountability to the argument that domesticating animals has at its core a real selfishness. In Jimmy's case, this was absolutely true. Animals can't tell us when they're in pain. Typically, given the option, cats and dogs will leave and find some place to die when the time comes. When they're confined, that dignity is kept from them. If you deny them that, you take on responsibility for any suffering they endure at being artificially kept alive. And what this client wanted was for me to humor and affirm his delusions about the normalcy of his situation—and the encouragement he took from his dog's sporadic, fleeting improvements. It wasn't cynical, and I didn't resent him for it. He just wasn't ready.

As a caregiver, and someone reasonably confident in the capacity of adults to handle certain difficult truths, I generally came down on the side of compassion for nonhumans in the face of human obliviousness. More than once, I gently advised clients that it was, perhaps, time to let go. Thankfully, that never blew up in my face. This case was different. Having interacted with this client somewhat regularly and spent enough time in his apartment to survey his books and other various tastes, I deduced two significant things. First, he was firmly in the closet. Second, it would be charitable to say this fact had *radically* constrained his social life. Jimmy was very likely the most substantive day-to-day relationship he had. Letting go of him was not simply letting go of an animal companion, it was letting go of a refuge; one that allowed for an otherwise untenable authenticity and depth of character—that allowed for feeling fully *seen*.

Quite literally, the *only* thing that can be said with 100 percent accuracy and consistency when we speak of relationships is the one thing none of us ever really wants to confront: *they end*. Always. Every single one of them. Arguably, it's their defining feature. In human relationships, it's probably more common that things come undone in some abrupt break or a drifting apart. But the best-case scenario is that a relationship is successful and rewarding for such a duration that one of the people involved simply dies. That's actually as good as it gets; the target we aim for, ostensibly.

I realize this isn't breaking news. That said, judging by the volume of artistic output devoted to mourning these endings (to say nothing of the mess of human drama that unfolds in response to them), it hardly seems foregone that humans have fully digested it, or that it figures in the foreground of most people's decision making. The fact is, as philosopher Judith Butler illustrates in a downright *gorgeous* passage in the opening chapter of her work *Undoing Gender*, as selves, we are socially constituted. That is, our self as we understand it exists in *relation* to others; an image culled from bouncing signals off a constellation of the familiar. Be that people, places, routines, sounds, or animal friends. Hence, mourning. That exhausting disorientation isn't simply a matter of sadness at *loss*. It's that in that loss, *we* have been irrevocably changed against our will, and time is required to adjust to whatever new self results.

Following a surgery during which famed Palestinian poet Mahmoud Darwish died and was then revived on the operating table, he penned a lengthy poem titled *Mural*, reflecting on selfhood in the face of glaring impermanence. Its closing lines almost propose an ethics for living:

> *And my name, though I mispronounce it over the coffin, is mine.*
> *As for me, filled with every reason to leave,*
> *I am not mine.*
> *I am not mine.*
> *I am not mine.*

Consciously being in relationship with others, as opposed to being in relation simply as a passive, inert fact of existence, is to consciously acknowledge we are not strictly our own. It's letting go of parts of our selves that reside in others. It's knowingly accepting the nonnegotiability of expiration dates, and that they will take from us not only those familiar to us or loved by us, but the selves we've come to know and with which we've become dexterous. Those will—with some regularity—exit stage, never to return. The only choice we'll have is in how fully we show up to that.

There is an *extraordinary* courage in that showing up. And because we're so susceptible to discounting the inevitability of endings, and relating to them as these disruptive, unjust anomalies in a narrative with some *other* thematic arc—I don't think we really give ourselves credit for what we have to summon just in order to *be with each other*. Something of that is stolen in vows of "till death do us part." Being together is not an "in the meantime" thing. It's a "one day you are going to die and one day I am going to die, and this moment is all we fucking have" affair. The fact that we perceive something so vital and valuable that we sign up for inevitable loss, disjuncture, and all that comes with both without recoiling in absolute horror—and that we will do it multiple times over—is nothing short of breathtaking.

With human relationships, lifespans are such that endings tend to figure as abstractions so distant as to be imponderable. With nonhumans, especially those of which people tend to be fond, the endpoints are keenly concrete. A decade or so. Maybe two, if nature's feeling generous. If I did my job well, it meant I'd be around when animals I worked with died. I knew that going in, every time. On a first foray out into the world together, I'd quietly acknowledge to both myself and the dog that I would likely experience their passing. And I would do so smiling. Because that was the best-case scenario.

The courage we summon in signing up to watch another person die, and in summoning that anew with each beginning, is magnified in human-animal relationships. And my admiration for clients in showing up to that undertaking was *fierce*. With some of them, I went through *generations* of companions they adopted and lost and adopted again. That resilience, that unfazed persistent devotion to discovering and falling in love with strangers over and over again, left me stunned and humbled. Every. Single. Time.

This left my walks with Jimmy wrought, and left me feeling hogtied and mute with relation to his human. Each day, each time I punched my security code into that building, I felt as though I were taking up an unworkable ball of knots; a series of mutually unsat-

isfactory options—all of which I was mostly powerless to improve.
The yawning gap between the world as it is and the world as it ought
to be has never been more of an acute experience for me than in
those agonizing moments where power, institutional inertia, and
happenstance conspire against someone's desire to simply *love well*.
It is rage inducing, in every instance. With any development or decision enacted in our lives—social, political, economic, whatever—
it seems fundamental to me that that metric ought to be applied:
how does this enable people to love well?

As far as I'm concerned, *anything* that obstructs or inhibits that
capacity ought to be burned to the fucking ground, no questions
asked, if for no other reason than that when the curtain begins to
draw on the short lives we race through, little else will have mattered. All other ends to which social forces bend are irrelevant in
its absence.

26

EXIT INTERVIEW

So I'm just gonna ask: Why'd you quit?
The easy answer is that the job was never particularly intellectually challenging, and anyone doing it knows that. You do it well, lock in a fairly localized and stable client base, and that's really *it*. After that, it's just repetition and maintenance, and provided you're nominally charismatic and not a complete fuckup, the latter mostly takes care of itself. Once you hit that autopilot, there's no getting around that it offers few opportunities for really pushing the life of one's mind.

Toward the end of my freelancing days, I realized I'd pretty much hit the ceiling on that front. I could go the entrepreneurial route, and "get creative" with engineering other people's exploitation and squeezing greater volumes of surplus value from their labor as a boss (and then maybe eventually *sell* that business). Or I could go the route that I did, putting my politics into conversation with this trade I'd learned, and create something that would expand democratic prospects as it grew. Beyond that, there wasn't really a move available to me that wasn't strictly lateral. And you know—*as it should be*, at least in the economic sphere. A commitment to arrangements of equality and democracy necessarily comes with certain tangible, material limits. I never really had the conversation with myself that goes *I'll never make more than this*, because I didn't need to. In a sane world, none of us should; certainly not at the expense of others. I felt enormously fortunate at having carved out the situation I had, for myself. And wanting more than that—on any front—felt like looking a gift horse in the mouth.

But over the years, my tastes changed, and I got more and more restless to be intellectually engaged in things that had real *stakes*.

So you walked away to pursue more challenging options?

Eh, the picture is a bit messier than that, and far less romantic. I'd spent fifteen years in D.C.—a notoriously transient city in a lot of ways. So, every few years, the landscape changed and I had a different arrangement of peers. There were steadily fewer "lifers" around; most lasted maybe four years. People would cycle out, new people would cycle in, activist and organizing formations would come and go, and all of it yielded subtle but nonetheless significant transformations. What I didn't really take into account was how that stacked the deck against the functioning of experience and institutional memory. The radical landscape was always getting younger, newer. And because much of that was happening well *after* the high-profile organizing and mass actions that followed the 1999 Seattle uprising, it came with a lot of self-convinced ro-mance. There were fewer and fewer people around to testify to the gritty, long-haul work that went into the storied things that had drawn younger activists to the District. Especially as social media came into prominence, it was enough to simply announce to your networks that you'd *done* something. Its effects were, at best, an afterthought.

So, for example, whereas the spring of 2000 saw 30,000 people take to the streets of downtown D.C. against the IMF and World Bank meetings, putting the words "structural adjustment" into the mainstream press probably more times than they had appeared in the previous quarter century—an enormous feat of coalition-build-ing, skill-cultivation, and strategy—within a decade those meetings were met with fifty folks wielding torches and nonspecific slogans, on a march through residential streets nowhere near either institu-tion, seemingly unaware of their resemblance to racist lynch mobs. Radical politics was kinda reduced to a "fake it till you make it" mentality. And because of the city's transience, and the (perhaps perfectly understandable) unwillingness of folks who'd done im-portant work to stick around—that tendency just went uncontested most of the time, and became more and more convinced of its own efficacy, despite pretty apparent diminishing returns.

And rather stupidly, I remained driven by this intense identi-fication with a "home" that no longer existed, and for which fewer and fewer people shared my sense of loss. Worse, the landscape I wanted to create and contribute to had been foreclosed on probably long before I even noticed. So continuing to fight for it made for a really toxic, acrimonious relationships. It never actually occurred to me that I might grow or change in ways that made D.C. a bad fit, and reaching that stage in life where you recognize not *everything* is achievable or within your control is mostly a matter of time. After beating my head against a wall for probably half a decade, I took a look around and realized that, if my happiness mattered—and as I've gotten older, it's mattered more and more—I needed to step out of my comfort zone and seek out other things.

But that's about place, not dog walking, really.
No, no. Totally. And when I left, I had no intention of quitting the trade, actually. I'd been toying with the idea of moving elsewhere, for about a year—but somewhere I could continue working in the trade. I was actually genuinely enticed by the challenge of building a new client base somewhere else, and the prospect of building a co-operative workplace with different parameters, different demands, different challenges (all with the benefit of previous trial and er-ror)—as well as just the opportunity to pursue new things outside my day job.

I'd actually considered Buenos Aires, for a bit, and was tenta-tively researching a possible move there. A friend had introduced me to Naomi Klein and her partner Avi Lewis a few times, explain-ing that I'd been inspired by their documentary *The Take*, about Argentine worker self-management following the 2001 financial collapse, and they'd offered to make virtual introductions for me

with their contacts there, if I wanted. That would've made for an
enormous opportunity to really deepen my engagement with democratic workplaces, even if I never came back to dog walking. At
the same time, I'd been coming and going from New York with
more frequency, attending conferences, speaking on panels, visiting friends. I loathed Manhattan, but Brooklyn felt more human
scaled, and relationships I'd formed there were taking up more and
more space in my internal life. If nothing else, a number of my fa-
vorite people from D.C. had moved there, and the idea of rebooting
my life with those relationships at the center was incredibly appeal-
ing. Then one day, a professor and sort of mentor of mine invited
me to squat a graduate course he was guest-teaching at The New
School, and it suddenly felt like time to pull the trigger.

So you just picked up and left?
Not entirely. I had met this other dog walker up there, through
neighbors of mine in D.C., and she'd asked if I had any interest in
subbing her holiday clients, since she was skipping the rush and going home to see family for a change. Anticipating how lucrative that
would be, the contacts it would generate, and the cushion it would
give me for establishing a foothold in New York, I jumped on it, and
moved my shit into an apartment just off the Brooklyn side of the
Manhattan Bridge. The first month or so, I was still working clients
in D.C. during the week and "living" in Brooklyn on the weekends.
A month or so in, she told me all but one of her holiday clients had
cancelled. All of a sudden, rather than seamlessly phasing out of

one city and into another, I was straddling the space between them, well and truly fucked. And what followed was the ass-kicking of my life.

What do you mean?

For starters, New York is a *much* bigger place. Just geographically. So scaling up something like a dog-walking outfit is incredibly difficult and slow going. Regardless of the city, the odds your initial clients are going to be concentrated in the same neighborhood are pretty slim. In D.C., that was a matter of clients being maybe four miles apart—in the worst case. New York City feels larger than some European *countries.* My first client was on West Twentieth, near the Flatiron. My second was on East Eighty-First Street. My third and fourth clients were in Park Slope. To make that work time-wise, I was beginning in the Flatiron District, biking up the West Side bike path to avoid lights, then cutting east on West Seventy-Seventh, racing cars through the Seventy-Ninth Street transverse in Central Park, then up to East Eighty-First. From there, I would bike the roughly ten miles down Second Avenue, across the Manhattan Bridge, and down Flatbush to Park Slope. It was categorically *insane,* and it kicked the living *shit* out of me. Living in Brooklyn, I was biking probably thirty miles for a client base worth maybe eighty dollars a day, initially. If I blew a tire or something, everything snarled and got royally fucked. But I didn't have any other choice. It was quite literally a matter of survival.

At the same time, wealth in New York City is a thing of real obscenity, and it produces a completely different culture and psychology than what one finds in D.C. The biggest assholes you're going to encounter in D.C. are either war criminals or enterprising, right-wing, bootstrap shitbags who pride themselves on their economization of *everything*. The average war criminal is almost *definitely* adjuncting at Georgetown, and lives out of some corporate temporary living suite, sans-dog. That leaves you the *other* breed of monster. If you provide a quality service for even a fraction less than a competitor, his very identity is bound up in hiring you. In New York? Conspicuous consumption is a very real thing. The first consultation I ever did there began with the building's elevator opening into the client's dining room. When they moved, I saw flyers for the apartments they were viewing—rents running from $10,000 to $15,000 monthly. For a not insignificant number of people, the performance of status that comes with dropping $100 a day on doggie daycare in Gramercy is its own reward. They don't care about spending less, or whether you're doing better work. It's a completely different sport, and the skills and intuition I'd cultivated in D.C. were effectively useless in the face of that.

So what happened?

I'd spent about a year desperately scraping together a client base in New York, and by about October of 2011, I'd finally gotten my head above water. Things were growing in such a way that I was en route to breaking my work into two routes and apprenticing someone to take one of them, so as to create more localized client concentrations. But I was also pretty battered. To cut down expenses, I'd illegally subletted my apartment and moved into a shithole place on South Third in Williamsburg, where a friend had a spare room. The courtyard area was basically the building's trash collection area, and there was no air-conditioning, so in the hotter months, the place reeked from rotting garbage wafting up and into the open windows. There was a water leak of some sort directly above the upper half of my bed, so each night I'd brush damp fallen plaster dust off of it, and then shower off whatever landed on me in my sleep the next morning. Our super's kid broke in and relieved me of my laptop. My cat died. The fact that work was finally turning around was really the only thing going well.

Then, at the end of the year, without any notice whatsoever, two of my biggest clients (one of whom had multiple walks a day) abruptly suspended service, on account of *both* having just brought home newborns. I started 2012 with my newly stable income nearly halved. It wasn't the end of the world, but it was a *huge* setback. And I was already only *just* catching my breath.

It sounds like you were in fight mode, though, anyway. Was that enough to throw your confidence?
No. Not really. But the fact that I got no advance notice of it, despite that newborns are hardly unanticipated, seemed worth noticing. In both cases, I found out when *I* contacted the clients to confirm their schedules. For them, it was an afterthought. It wasn't as though I'd performed poorly, or some interpersonal fissure precipitated it.

These were people with whom I was on really good terms; people who added me on Facebook in some cases. So the lack of consideration—even if totally unintentional—felt foreboding.

At the same time, Occupy Wall Street had been underway for months, and the encampment had been evicted from Zuccotti Park only a few weeks prior. I'd been neck deep in it, pulling various duties in the education and empowerment working group and consulting a little with efforts to launch worker-cooperatives out of other working groups, as well as participating in the neighborhood assemblies the movement had spun off in the outer boroughs—specifically Occupy Williamsburg and Occupy Brooklyn. I'd been on the Brooklyn Bridge during the showdown with the NYPD back in October, which was probably the first thing that really got the mainstream's attention, and I'd thus become a go-to source for a few journalists. I'd also been solicited to write on what was happening, for various movement websites. Occupy was *the* story in the mainstream, at that point, and was increasingly *the* national story, as well.

The publication of and breakout bestseller numbers on David Graeber's *Debt: The First 5,000 Years* had also lent a certain new legitimacy to the distinctly anarchist politics coming out of Occupy. So those of us who were versed in prior, similar grassroots movements and could provide context for what was unfolding were taken a *lot* more seriously. A whole generation of journalists cropped up, almost overnight. People I'd met in the park before the eviction wound up writing for *Rolling Stone*, Al Jazeera, and other mainstream outlets. Suddenly, I had opportunities to exercise faculties and skillsets I'd back-burnered for a number of years, and in really engaging contexts. There was a real and materially substantive demand for knowledge production around radical politics and the like. And thus, there were outlets for doing that that weren't dependent upon my bending my day job toward political ends.

And amid all that, a number of my movement mentors were encouraging me to step back from things and devote real time to just *writing*. So it wasn't so much that the income setback threw my confidence in some determinative way. Other passions were creeping into the foreground, from my periphery, and I guess I was just a lot less single-minded about primary commitments.

So what was it that gave you the final shove?
Sometime in January, when I was already skipping meals to account for the sudden lost income, I biked through a midday of that shitty, not-quite-freezing rain typical of the season, to my only remaining Upper East Side client. She lived on the sixth floor of a walkup near the Met. The climb was a routine feature of my day, but that particular day, I was spent from stress, undereating, and biking anywhere had become almost unbearable thanks to some bilateral nerve issue that left me with excruciating pain in my upper arms for weeks at a time. At that point, I'd assumed it was just my body telling me I was nutrient deficient, which just kind of spit into the overall wound that my life had become. Working scattered off-time walks or overnight gigs was my only salvation those months, and because

those were often a vector for new midday clients, taking an evening job somewhere was an opportunity cost I couldn't afford. So I was kinda confined to this course that was breaking me down on a daily basis. Climbing those stairs off Lexington was like this ritual walking meditation on how miserable I was.

I'd been mulling, for some time, the fact that D.C. clients had regularly texted or called me to warn me of changes or contingencies that had no bearing on me whatsoever—a potted plant was moved, or something comparably insignificant. While in New York, two clients had just shrugged at the option of giving me any advance notice on schedule changes that would cost me upward of $1,200 a month. I was probably mulling that very contrast as I climbed those stairs that day. So when I reached my client's landing and found a refrigerator in front of her door, something in me just fucking *broke*.

I pretty quickly figured out that she'd put it out there for the super or some other person to retrieve. She had fostered this rescued pit bull and had fallen so in love with him that she just kept him. But he was still a pit bull, and people were irrationally afraid of him. Clearly, her fridge had shit the bed, needed to be replaced, and the super or whoever was scared to go into her apartment without her there. The problem was that moving refrigerators was pretty squarely outside my job description. If she'd locked a deadbolt for which I didn't have a key, it'd have been out of my hands that I couldn't walk her dog. This was only different in that I was staring at an oversized home appliance that doubled as a sort of absurdist "fuck you," doubling down on the lack of consideration I'd been mulling over for several weeks. The takeaway seemed to be that, in a city of 8.5 million people, there's a sort of learned self-effacing that happens. Virtually no one assumes that what they do in any given moment *matters*. Inversely, no one assumes that what they *don't* do matters. And in whatever fight lay ahead of me, possibly one every bit as soul crushing as the last year had been, that would be a factor. There would be more costly afterthoughts from clients. There would be more refrigerators.

Standing on that landing, exhausted, soaked in freezing rain, my arms aching so badly I wanted to die . . . I just decided I was *done*.

Wait. So that was it? The refrigerator?
Yep.

Isn't that a little . . . drastic? Silly? Petty, even? I mean, you're talking about a career that had, at least for some time, treated you really well.
Maybe. It's not as though I arrived at all of this without some self-examination. I *chose* to be there, in those particular conditions. At every stage up to that moment, I had made certain decisions. Many of which may have been grave errors. Certainly, I'd misjudged any number of risks I'd taken. I could've made entirely *other* decisions. I have no doubt someone smarter than me would've gone about it other ways. And none of this is to say that I took the fortune I'd

enjoyed for a full *decade* in that line of work for granted. I was exceedingly aware of the manner in which I'd cheated despair and boredom the whole time. Honestly, it felt like a fucking heist, most days.

But from where I was standing in that moment, the one thing that had kept me in the trade, that kept me from—speaking strictly pragmatically—monetizing other skills, was that dog walking was so much less risky, so much less stressful. I could make a comfortable living and sleep soundly each night knowing that I didn't have to worry about how the following day might make or break my material well-being, or how someone could pull the whole rug out from under me arbitrarily. It didn't come with all the unknowns and precarity that other careers did. The tradeoff was that it wouldn't ever likely yield any meaningful accomplishment, either. Its joys and victories were quiet, modest, and mostly private.

The fact was: *it was no longer taking care of me.* I didn't claim any definitive knowledge of why that was. It's quite possible that I just couldn't hack it and got in over my head rolling the dice in New York. Such explanations—whatever their content—weren't altogether useful to me, in that moment. All I could really think was, If I've gotta entertain this kind of instability and deprivation, there are far more interesting ways of doing that. I didn't have any other prospects looming, so I resolved to keep working my remaining clients until something else presented itself. But it was strictly a survival strategy. I was no longer committed to staying in it or making it work.

How much longer were you at it?

My memory of that day is hazy, now, so I don't really recall exactly how much longer I worked. I know my last day in the field was mid-March 2012.

So, presumably, something else came up that allowed you to bail out.

Sort of, yeah. Being on the board of the Institute for Anarchist Studies, I'd had my hand in a number of publishing projects in the previous years. I'd provided some limited editorial consultation on a couple books in a series we curated with AK Press, and I'd edited most of this pamphlet series we'd done targeting younger activists when Occupy kicked off—which proved wildly popular. Another board member worked as a freelance editor and copyeditor, professionally, and got pitched an editing gig that she couldn't take on. So she recommended me. It was a *massive* manuscript, and the author had a budget of a few grand to get it down to roughly half the size of the draft he handed off. It was more money than I'd seen at one time in *years*.

During those very same weeks, Will Potter—an investigative journalist out of the animal-rights movements, covering state repression and criminalization of activists—also contacted me. Ironically, we'd met because I'd once walked his dog. A German publication had commissioned him to do a piece on the state's response to the Occupy movement, and they wanted photos to go with it. I'd been pretty prolific in photographing the movement, so he asked if he could use some of what I'd produced. In exchange,

the magazine was offering more than what I'd paid for the iPhone
I'd used to shoot the photos.

*But that couldn't have really paid much more than walking dogs at
that point, right? So you were still in the same boat, no?*
Yeah. Similar numbers, and more irregular, but it enabled greater
mobility. My mom had been asking me to visit her in Spain, and a
friend in Jerusalem had been inviting me to stay in her guest room
for months. Having an income that didn't bind me to a particular
geography, I moved out of the shithole on South Third, and headed
across the Atlantic. By April, I was talking anarchism and Occupy
to audiences in Greece. By June, I was doing the same in London
and Lancaster. In between, I interviewed anarchists in the West
Bank for a magazine out of Beirut, picked up editing for a couple
freelance journalists, and ghostwrote a term paper for a grad student in Geneva. It wasn't steady work, and I was struggling in many
of the same ways I had been the prior year, but I also saw the Islamic
tile art of the Alhambra that inspired Escher's best work, climbed a
thousand year old mosque in Cairo, and somehow wound up having coffee opposite Mandy Patinkin in Ramallah.

The fact that I can say any of that out loud feels light years from
staring at that fucking refrigerator.

Do you miss it?
Absolutely. Look, there's no job I can think of that combines its particular elements. I'm honestly not sure it *gets* better than someone
paying you to amble about early-summer Crown Heights with an

iced coffee and two dogs acting out their own excited wonder at the world between approval-seeking over-the-shoulder glances. Like, are you *kidding* me? I would pick that over reading spy novels on a beach in Thailand, any day of the week. And I've never even *been* to Thailand.

And to be totally honest, I've done some pet care by request here and there, since "retiring." I've pet-sat for friends and family in Oakland, Naples, Istanbul, and Ramallah, and even pinch-hit for a friend with a freelance route in Brooklyn a few days a week, one summer. I also did some consulting and training work for a nonprofit that was helping launch an immigrant-run cooperative dog-walking agency in Sunset Park, Brooklyn. I've never really gotten it out of my system, and I'm not sure I *want* to. A lot of my friends are still dog walkers, and our day-to-day banter has a certain knowing to it that comes from our shared DNA there. At the end of the day, whatever adventures my life's afforded me, it's impossible *not* to miss rolling out of bed, throwing on jeans, a hoodie, and slip-ons, and showing up for no one but *dogs*.

The only world I'm interested in fighting for is one in which *everyone's* life is that rewarding. I say that quite seriously.

Acknowledgments

I owe James Birmingham, Jay Cassano, and Nathan Schneider an enormous thanks for nudging this into fruition and Cindy Milstein for being tireless in her support and encouragement. The same goes for Dennis Johnson at Melville House, for having any faith whatsoever that I'd pull this off. Along the way, Jaime Taylor, Nick Pimentel, and Christy Thornton provided me with crucial research assistance. Atheer Yacoub, Reuben Blanchard, Welch Canavan, and Kotu Bajaj delivered priceless feedback as readers, and Mark Krotov exerted ninja-level sarcasm in the process, both as my editor and my chief Twitter distraction. A great deal of thanks goes to Willow and Harjit in Oakland, Karla and Joseph in Istanbul, Mira in Utrecht, Breezy in Los Angeles, and my mom in Napoli—all of whose homes served as sort-of writing retreats, usually while I pet-sat their little ones and drank their coffee.

ABOUT THE AUTHOR

Joshua Stephens's writing has appeared in *AlterNet, Truthout, NOW* (Lebanon), *Jadaliyya,* and *Perspectives on Anarchist Theory.*